UNRETIRED

Praise for Unretired

"*Unretired* will empower you to pursue joy in today's shifting workplace and have a positive impact on others in a chapter of life filled with unlimited potential. It's a treasure trove of personal stories, in-depth interviews and pragmatic advice with more than a dollop of inspiration!"

> —**KERRY HANNON**, Yahoo Finance Senior Columnist and bestselling author of *In Control at 50+* and *Great Jobs for Everyone 50+.*

"My goal was to retire at age 59. Mission accomplished! However, loss of identity and meaning was a real problem for me. Mark S. Walton's book, *Unretired,* explains why I, and so many others like me, feel the need to stay engaged. Read his book—it will show you how to successfully navigate the new world of unretirement!"

> —**KEVIN TROUT**, Chair, Vistage Worldwide, host, *Three Rivers Leadership* podcast and owner, Grandview Insights LLC.

"Wow! What a great read. Kept me hungry for more. We've been told that all we need for a successful retirement is sufficient financial means, but it's a myth. This book tells the truth—what we need, no matter our age, is sufficient purpose and a sense of accomplishment. *Unretired* puts the spotlight where it belongs. Read this intelligent book and start planning how you will invest *yourself* going forward.

> —**MITCH ANTHONY**, financial industry advisor, podcaster and author of *The New Retirementality.*

"What makes some of us want to keep working well past traditional retirement age? Mark Walton has studied and visited with people who keep on going, and discovered why they do it. The stories he tells and advice he provides in *Unretired* will help you think about your own life, career and plans for the future."

> —**MARK MILLER**, *New York Times* contributing columnist, publisher of RetirementRevised.com and author, *Retirement Reboot.*

"To those considering retiring: Stop! Think long and hard. Mark S. Walton's book, *Unretired,* packed with psychology, neuroscience, practical guidance and scores of personal stories comes as a revelation. Read this book—you'll view your own life's potential with a fresh eye."

> —**BARBARA BRADLEY HAGERTY**, *New York Times* bestselling author of *Fingerprints of God* and contributing writer to *The Atlantic.*

Published by Profit Research Inc.

Unretired/Mark S. Walton-1st ed. February 2024 Trade Paperback

Paperback: 978-1-7360094-0-6
Ebook: 978-1-7360094-2-0

UNRETIRED

How Highly
Effective People
Live Happily
Ever After

MARK S. WALTON

profit research inc.
Established 1958 • New York

For Jane,

Forever my Managing Editor

CONTENTS

Retirement is the filthiest word in the language. Whether by choice or fate, to retire from what you do—and what makes you what you are—is to back up into the grave.

—ERNEST HEMINGWAY

Who Flunks Retirement?

The day I spoke with my friend Vito Maggiolo about his retirement plans, he was in a fire department vehicle with lights flashing outside a Washington D.C. apartment building where an electrical panel had exploded.

It was a Saturday afternoon in April and the fire chief was worried about the safety of the building's residents, as well as wind gusts spreading smoke and flames onto the street.

He was right to be concerned—this was a heavily trafficked part of town.

But Vito wasn't even slightly fazed.

His job as chief spokesman for the city's fire and emergency medical services department was to alert local and national news outlets and, through them, the public, to brewing dangers and developments.

It was a 24/7 high-stress position that he had transitioned into at age 65, and one for which he had been thoroughly trained, he told me, and even dreamed about as a kid.

> *Like I said in my job interview: "Let me get this right. You're gonna give me a red car with a light and a siren, and you're gonna tell me to chase fires, and you're gonna pay me for it?"*
>
> *But, joking aside, it can get very intense. I respond to any working fire or any incident that has potential media interest. So, at three o'clock in the morning, I'm often up and at it.*

Other than a propensity for sleeping lightly, what capabilities are called for in a job like Vito's?

Knowledge and know-how; organizational, problem solving and communication skills; and the wherewithal to analyze and juggle significant amounts of incoming information, on deadline and under heavy pressure.

The same abilities, in fact, that he'd developed and relied on in his previous 35-year career as an assignment editor and producer in the Washington bureau of Cable News Network, a job that can burn out even the steeliest individual in less than half the time.

Vito explained:

The assignment desk was the center of activity in the newsroom. It was a constant whirlwind. My job was having 20 field crews move to respond to breaking news situations. So, it was always an intense experience.

I was in that position for the Ronald Reagan assassination attempt, for 9/11 and the attack on the Pentagon, during the Monica Lewinsky grand jury proceedings and a long list of major news events.

Outside Washington, the roles that Vito had successfully undertaken were not only challenging but often dangerous, as during Operation Desert Storm, the American and allied invasion of Iraq.

Within a week or so after the beginning of the air war, Saddam Hussein agreed to allow CNN to return and do live television. I was tasked as the producer who led the team back into Iraq.

And I remained there for 40 days and nights until we were ordered out again. During that time was the air war, the remainder of the ground war and then the U.S. troops coming into Baghdad.

Given the exceedingly interesting life that he had led for so many years, and how well he was suited for it, I was surprised when, speaking with me from that downtown

Washington fire scene, Vito told me that he was thinking about chucking it all, cold turkey.

His plan was to move to New Orleans, a city he'd come to enjoy while on news assignments, and somewhere he felt that he could kick back and relax—a place where he could enjoy the music, dancing, local food and not having to wake up on a schedule.

"It's just a matter of deciding when I want to pull the trigger," he said. "I'll spend time in the fire house, which is a great social outlet for me, but I truly feel that I'm capable of stepping down from my current state of mind and readjusting to retirement. I feel very comfortable in my assessment of myself."

Will Vito's retirement play out as he thinks? Partying at night, waking up late, filling his days with friends and relaxation?

Perhaps, but I seriously doubt it.

My guess is that, after a few months or a year, at most, he will be mindlessly bored, miss the stimulation of his working years and be actively seeking ways to extend or reinvent his career in yet another way.

I predict this, not only because I personally know how effective and accomplished Vito is but, more importantly, based on the research and in-depth interviews with the unretired people you will meet in this book.

THE MOTIVATION TO KEEP WORKING

The pages ahead are not about personal finances or shoring up a nest egg.

Like Vito, a good number of the people you will meet had acquired sufficient assets to live comfortably for the rest of their years; others valued the idea of generating additional income to pay for luxuries or enhanced lifestyles; still others hadn't yet attained these financial freedoms but were working their way toward them.

[Money aside, what motivated them all to keep working, not just for a few more years, but well beyond the time when most people call it quits, was a fascination with the nature of their work, a continuing sense of joy and excitement from it, and a drive to have a positive impact on others.]

What's the personal makeup of people such as these—the characteristics of those who tend to never retire, or after giving retirement a try, head back to work?

Sometimes even run?

A combination of several, or all, of the following words best describes them:

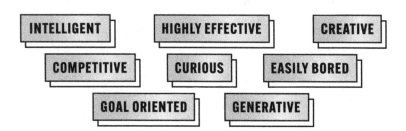

INTELLIGENT   HIGHLY EFFECTIVE   CREATIVE

COMPETITIVE   CURIOUS   EASILY BORED

GOAL ORIENTED   GENERATIVE

Today, there are tens of millions of career professionals with these attributes who have reached, are approaching, or have begun to seriously think about their so-called "retirement years."

If you're reading this book, this likely includes you.

If you were born any time after the Second World War, you are part of America's first generation to earn a living in today's *knowledge economy,* a still emerging paradigm in which the keys to success are education, information, technology and your personal effectiveness in utilizing them.

[Because as a knowledge professional, you've structured your life and built your career with your *mind*, rather than muscles, you may find it difficult, if not impossible, to power down your brain and be content with a lifestyle that does not inherently provide the kind of challenges and stimulation to which you've become accustomed]

Simply put, even if you've looked forward to it for years, and even if you can afford to kick back and relax forevermore, there's a significant chance—better than a 50% likelihood—that you will fail while trying.

What then?

Where is the path to living happily ever after for those of us who instinctively fear that we will, or have already flunked retirement?

In many instances, knowledge professionals find out the hard way.

RETIRED BY ACCIDENT

Jim DeMartini, M.D., a Sonoma County, California radiologist with four decades of experience, had always been passionate about his work.

In the 1980s, when he completed his training, the first clinical CT scanners were becoming widely available, elevating radiology from a useful medical tool to a practice that, with the advent of other new imaging technologies, became crucial in the diagnosis and treatment of cancer and other diseases.

"You use your knowledge directly day to day," he told me. "It's like solving mysteries, something you can do to immediately help the patient, to put him in the right direction. It's very rewarding, a little stressful because you really have to say to yourself: *I can't make a mistake, because if I do, the patient suffers.*"

Shortly after his 72nd birthday, Jim suddenly found himself retired. One day he was working his usual eight to ten hour, six-day-a-week schedule, and the next day he wasn't.

It's not uncommon, unfortunately, for experienced professionals to find themselves, without warning or recourse, ushered or forced out the door sooner than they had anticipated.

In Jim's case, however, it was not a push, but rather a breakdown in communication that turned him into an unsuspecting retiree.

> *Most of the people in my group retired in their mid to late 60s, and I just kept going because I still liked it. And then the radiology group I was in decided to hire several new doctors, and I said: "Listen, if you have enough people, I'll retire, because I don't want you to have too many on staff."*
>
> *They interpreted that as meaning that I wanted to retire, so it's kind of an accident that I retired in the first place. At some point I looked down at my schedule for the next month and I wasn't on it, so I knew I had retired!*

Jim decided to make the best of it. He'd done well financially, had no real need for the continuing income from his job and, over the years, had formulated a plan for what he would do when he retired, whenever that occurred, which he put into action.

Living in northern California provided him with the best of all worlds for the year-round outdoor activities he had always enjoyed on his days off: golfing, cycling, hiking and windsurfing in the summer, and skiing in the nearby mountains in winter.

He now dove into all these sports with gusto, hoping his free time would allow him to significantly boost his performance. But at his age, he soon found that any gains were only modest.

As a result, he shifted his attention to indoor activities, painstakingly following nearly every recommendation in the most popular retirement planning books:

I started taking classes at the local college, I started a book group with a bunch of other radiologists, and I also took some painting lessons.

So that was my approach, that I was gonna do all these things. I volunteered to teach at a nearby medical school. I checked all the boxes. And my days were full— it wasn't like I suddenly retired and had no other life.

"This is what you're supposed to do in retirement," I told myself, but I kept thinking: "What am I doing?" It was just this feeling that I was useless.

It just felt empty, that's the best term for me, so empty.

After months of frantically trying to adapt to a life that he found meaningless and unsustainable, he finally admitted to himself that he'd reached a turning point.

I'm playing golf with guys whose idea of a perfect day is to come out to the golf course, play golf and then play a round of dominoes and get back home around 4 p.m.

This is the San Francisco Bay area, mind you, so most of these guys had been in finance, law or medicine, so it wasn't like they worked for a big corporation that had burned them out. But this was their idea of a great life, this was it, this was great.

[Me, I had a valuable skill and I wanted to be a contributing member of society.]

So Jim did just what you might expect: after contacting his former office, where he learned that even with the beefed-up staff there was still an overload of patients, he headed back to work with a huge sense of relief.

At age 72-and-a-half, he once again became Jim DeMartini M.D., the guy who loves radiology.

A SEISMIC SHIFT

Jim's decision to keep working later in life is part of a significant but often underreported trend that has begun to impact nearly every corner of America's economy, as well as those of other developed nations.

Between the years 2021 and 2022, for example, despite the continuing coronavirus pandemic, nearly 10% of college-educated Americans aged 65 or older who had previously retired, changed their minds and rejoined the workforce.

Moreover, during the past few decades, the number of college graduates in this age group who decided to keep working, rather than retire, has more than quadrupled. And the numbers keep climbing—with hundreds of thousands more projected to join them in each year to come.

By the year 2030, the number of working 65-plus-year-old Americans with college or advanced degrees will be greater than the populations of Los Angeles and Chicago combined.

What's more, *people aged 75 and older*, at all educational levels, have recently become the fastest-growing part of the U.S. workforce, with the percentage of employed people in this group nearly doubling over the past three decades.

Reports the *Wall Street Journal*: "For many people, the idea of stopping work is a nonstarter—an inevitable path to boredom, ill health and a life devoid of meaning."

"We are entering an era of unretirement," wrote Ewan Thomson of the World Economic Forum in June 2023.

REBELS, REINVENTORS AND CREATIVES

The book before you is a journey, an expedition through the lives, thoughts and experiences of people between the ages of about 60 and 80, who have no interest in retiring, stepping back, dropping out or adjusting to a way of life that does not, and likely never will, make them truly happy.

My interviews with them were on the record; their stories and experiences are genuine; the questions that I posed are those I believe you would ask if you met them.

Their answers are candid, straightforward and, in every case, illuminating.

You will have more in common with some of them than with others. Nevertheless, they will prompt you to think about yourself, your career, the life you've led to this point and your plans for the future.

In Part One, *The Rebels,* we'll examine the most scientific study ever done on the pitfalls of retirement and visit first-hand with knowledge professionals, like radiologist Jim DeMartini, who managed to continue working in the same field they entered when they first graduated from college, graduate or professional school.

We'll also explore the brain science behind our potential to work happily and expertly for decades beyond what most people would expect.

In Part Two, *The Reinventors,* we'll examine the growing job and entrepreneurship market for unretirees, then focus on people, including former CEOs, who rejected the notion of retiring and instead radically reinvented their career tracks, taking on roles that mixed skills they had developed earlier with new interests and fascinations.

In Part Three, *The Creatives,* we'll get to know people, in their early 60s and beyond, who discovered within themselves creative skills and abilities they were never previously aware of. We'll learn how their sudden transformations occurred and what that may mean for the rest of us.

Additionally, we'll drop in on the new creative economy—an unshackled marketplace where you no longer need a technical degree to become a celebrated inventor, a gallery to be a nationally-known artist, or a TV show to be an on-camera star, no matter your age.

Throughout the book you will discover answers to questions we all should consider when deciding whether retirement or unretirement is the best choice for us as individuals—the *why, where, when and how* to make one of the most important decisions of our adult lives.

Questions like:

- Why Do People Flunk Retirement?
- What Are the Odds for Me Personally?
- When Do People Usually Unretire?

- What Role Does Money Play?
- What Kinds of Work Do They Do Next?
- Where Do They Find Such Work?
- What Are the Rewards and Paybacks?
- How Long Will My Brain Support a High-Level Career?
- How Do I Design an Unretirement Plan?

Only those who have personally experienced unretirement, and the experts who have studied them, can provide real-life, practical responses to such questions.

These are the individuals you will meet and hear from directly in *Unretired*.

This is a book for and about people who fundamentally reject the idea of leaving behind a life they have found satisfying and important in order to adjust to something less enjoyable and meaningful because society says "the time has come."

It's for those of us who, after due consideration, feel motivated to break with convention and change the map of life.

PART ONE

THE REBELS

CHAPTER ONE

A Tale of Two Psychologists

Once upon a time, somewhere around 2010, two widely respected research psychologists conducted what is considered the most sophisticated and comprehensive study ever done on the topic of retiring from work.

Interviewing nearly 1,500 retirees from all walks of life, they posed a series of meticulously crafted inquiries designed to elicit candid, extended responses to a central underlying question: *Now that you're no longer working, how are things going for you?*

Additionally, they interviewed 400 people of the same age and demographic characteristics who were still actively involved in their careers. The goal here was to understand this second group's expectations about retiring from work and compare them to the realities of retirement through a statistical method called regression analysis.

Along with their professional interests in all of this, the psychologists, Dr. Rob Pascale and Dr. Lou Primavera, each had a personal agenda at stake.

Rob, in his mid-50s at the time of the study, had recently stepped down as president of the powerhouse market research firm that he had founded, Marketing Analysts Inc., and was in search of the secrets of a long, happy retirement.

Lou, who was approaching age 70, in addition to his corporate consulting and teaching activities, was Associate Provost of Touro College in New York and was considering his future, as well.

Once the in-depth interviews were complete, and the responses cross-checked and analyzed, Rob and Lou wrote a scholarly summary of their discoveries, published by Rowman and Littlefield, known for releasing serious, academic books for more than 50 years.

The title chosen was: *The Retirement Maze: What You Should Know Before and After You Retire.*

Throughout the more than 200 pages filled with citations and detailed explanatory data, Rob and Lou's results were unmistakably clear and scientifically reaffirmed the findings of previous smaller studies:

Retiring from work is not right for everybody—in fact, for a solid majority of people, it can turn out to be a seriously bad idea.

Most retirees are reluctant to talk about this, Rob told me, for fear of sounding naïve, argumentative or personally flawed.

But, because their study guaranteed anonymity, their research subjects felt entirely comfortable, Rob explained, in telling it like it is:

I think the worst part of it, and the reason we wrote the book, is because people are not aware of the conditions you're going to face when you stop working. You're not aware that you're losing your friends, that what kind of job you had mattered. There are so many aspects to what happens in your life that there's no way you could ever know without being retired.

So that was one of the reasons we also wanted to interview people who were still working, to get their perspective. Watching these people gradually work their way toward leaving their careers was like previewing a train wreck—that's how I would describe it.

What the study underscored is that for many people, particularly those who enjoyed and were effective in their work lives, retirement is a stage of life filled with losses from which it can be difficult, if not impossible, to recover.

The most common of these losses are:

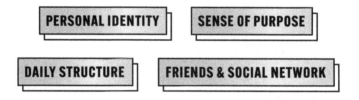

For nearly a century, since the concept of retirement was first popularized, retirement books, workshops and coaching programs have spread the notion that the voids left by these losses can and must be filled in order to adjust to the retirement lifestyle.

In fact, a huge retirement advice industry has grown up around the mantra that doing this is the "new job" of the retiree who has left his or her job or career behind.

But Rob and Lou's real-world research indicated that this is nothing more than a fool's errand, that the emptiness created by lack of meaningful work is not easily, if ever, overcome. And that the camaraderie and social connections built up over years in the workplace is something that can rarely be replaced

Rob explained:

Over time our research shows that only 44% of people ever consider themselves to be happy after they stop working.

One of the things we have when we retire is expectations that life will be this or that, but our expectations are driven by what we did in our lives, in our careers and how interesting or fulfilling and satisfying our careers were.

Now that's all gone and the idea that you can replace those things with personal interests, hobbies, or making new friends, proves to be false.

For instance, when you leave your job you lose half the number of people you were friends with. And even though you think you can make up for that, you really can't. You no longer have the same interests as they do.

Gradually, you move away from those people and spend much more time alone, not only because you know fewer people but because you're not in an environment that promotes social interaction.

So it's easy to get to a point where you finally say: "Ah, the hell with it, I'll just live with what I have, even though I'm unhappy and stuck in the middle of the maze."

That's the way it was for me.

Yes, you read that last line correctly; and it's an important part of the tale of Drs. Lou Primavera and Rob Pascale.

WHAT HAPPENED TO ROB?

As mentioned earlier, Rob was in his mid-50s when the study was done, and part of his motivation was to learn how to deal with the personal hopelessness he felt, having recently retired from his position as head of the marketing research firm he had founded decades before.

Instead, the study results served to confirm his greatest fear: that even though he could easily afford it, taking early retirement was one of the biggest mistakes he had ever made.

> *I definitely should have stayed at work at least a few more years. I could have found an alternate way to reduce the pressure, like work fewer hours or hire more people. There were alternatives that I could have done that probably would have worked out better.*

Rob experienced what he and Lou came to see, through their research, as an inevitable cycle for more than half of all retirees.

At first blush, everything seems great.

I woke up the morning after I retired with such a feeling of elation that I no longer had to deal with that stress every day. And I enjoyed it the first few weeks, because that's how the cycle works.

But then you realize, you know, I've got too many hours in the day.

And that's one of the things that really occurred to me—how many hours there are in a day to try to fill. Even now, I still go through the same thing. I look and it's three in the afternoon. Can we have dinner yet? Can we go to bed? It's kind of ridiculous.

But you go into these doldrums a few months into retirement, and you can stay there, possibly forever.

Rob tried painting, something he had previously loved as a hobby, and had plans to continue and expand after retiring. But things didn't work out as he'd hoped. After a short while, he found painting onerously boring and realized that it had simply been a temporary diversion from the daily stresses of his career.

Next, he followed the lead of other retired entrepreneurs, experimenting with new business ventures that seemed interesting to him because they involved products and services he wanted to learn more about.

He got involved in a company that imported organic foods, invested in a racehorse and opened a jewelry store.

Before long, however, he decided that he didn't want to put in the long, hard hours necessary to make these new businesses successful, so he shut them down.

He took dance lessons with his wife and traveled extensively.

"But you can never travel enough to fill a retirement life," he concluded. "If you're out 10 weeks a year, which is a lot of travel, you still have 42 weeks left to figure out what to do with yourself."

And what about a dozen years after retiring, when he hit his late 60s, the age at which I interviewed him for this book?

I'm still searching, I'm still looking. And I tell my friends who talk to me about retirement: "You're getting older, but milk that career as long as you can. Never, ever quit your job. Make them throw you out."

And that's the irony of this whole thing. I quit too early. What am I doing now? Talking to you about how miserable retirement is.

I wish I'd known back then what I know now.

WHAT HAPPENED TO LOU?

On the other hand, when I spoke with Lou Primavera, he had just passed his 80th birthday and was still at work in his chosen career, building on the kind of work he had found challenging for more than six decades.

Lou was the kind of person I refer to in this book as a *Rebel,* meaning that he was not only working well past the traditional retirement age, but had managed to remain in the same field he had entered on the day he graduated from college.

As you will find in the pages to come, this is considerably more feasible for people in certain kinds of professions, companies, or organizations—while people who don't fit this profile commonly create new structures or venues for themselves in order to be successfully unretired.

At age 80, Lou had a résumé highlighting "areas of specialization" that for most people, including me, would require a translator and a half-hour explanation to barely comprehend.

In addition to his position as Associate Provost at Touro College, he was actively involved in "univariate and multivariate statistics, psychometrics, test and survey construction, experimental design, scaling, stigma and discrimination in mental health."

The bottom line is that he was an expert in using complex psychological methodologies to study human and organizational behavior and develop ways to help people and teams improve the way they operate.

"I teach data analysis and research design," he told me. "I teach people how to do research studies, the kind of stuff you read about in the newspaper all the time. And I teach them how to do statistical analysis. Whenever you do research, you have to do statistical analysis to understand the results."

In our conversation, Lou credited the retirement study that he and Rob Pascale had completed a decade earlier for hardening his resolve to continue working as long as possible.

Reading through the research, he said, had generated a moment of absolute clarity.

> *There's always that initial elation, you know, when people retire. You're really happy at first, then, all of a sudden, and there's a very predictable cycle, you start to go down, down, down. And either you find a way up again or, if not, you're stuck at the bottom.*
>
> *I'm sure Rob told you that one of the things we found in the study was an increase in the use of antidepressants. Not surprising at all. Some people just fall apart. They accept the idea that there's no reason to do the kinds of things they used to do in their careers.*

[Seeing this in black and white, I thought to myself: "I like doing what I'm doing, so I'm gonna keep doing it. Do I need the money? No, but it's challenging me, it's having me learn new stuff. It makes me weary sometimes, upset sometimes, but would I give it up? Absolutely not."]

And what, I asked, would be his prescription, as a highly trained psychologist, for those of us who have reached or been pushed into retirement and are trying to find our way to happily ever after?

If you're a manual worker, eventually you have to be worn out. Let's say you're a bricklayer. Can you do that when you're 80? I don't think so. But that's different than most of us today.

[For those who work with our minds, rather than muscles, I think full-stop retirement is a major mistake. If you don't want to or are unable to continue doing what you've done, go do something else.]

I'm a psychologist, right? [So I tell you to select activities that maximize your strengths. Analyze your skills going back to your original job or career. Where do they fit? Where will you feel good about what you're doing?]

You've got to be willing to experiment, be willing to keep trying different things until you find something that's right for you. And then decide how to go about making it a part of your life and how you want to allocate your time.

Personally, I'm gonna go down fighting—that's what I have concluded.

That's what the rest of the happily unretired people you are about to meet concluded as well.

CHAPTER TWO

The Fascination Factor

When Alyce Shultz grew up on a Wisconsin dairy farm in the early 1940s, women who earned a college degree had three basic career choices.

"At that point in time, you could be a teacher, a nurse or a secretary" she told me, "I went on to be a nurse."

That's where the similarity ends between Alyce and nearly all her peers.

When we visited, just after her 80th birthday, she said she simply could not relate to the decision that most others had made years earlier—to retire.

I can't understand that life. My friends, and even one of my grandsons here always asks me: "Grandma when are you going to retire?"

Because, you know, I still work a fair amount. I have a friend who just contacted me and asked if I wanted to go on a seven week cruise. And I said: "I can't. I have all these things that I have to get done."

I think retired people age more quickly. They aren't necessarily people that I travel with. I sometimes wonder what they do all day. They would rather play golf, and I would rather go teach in South Africa.

Married right out of nursing school, Alyce gave birth and started raising a son and a daughter, while simultaneously jumping headfirst into a job in one of the nation's first open heart critical care units, located at the University of Wisconsin Medical Center.

She subsequently had two more daughters, moved multiple times and worked in almost every area of nursing—from hospital settings to home care, to private duty, to doctors' offices.

Then, in her late 40s, things fell apart—or perhaps jelled for the first time.

She came to realize that she had made two miscalculations that were impacting her happiness and well-being: she had stayed married to the wrong man for too long, and she had failed to follow her instincts about the direction of her career.

"What I really cared about, what fascinated me, was not the status quo but an opportunity to make change," she explained.

"I was still a nurse at heart, but I had always been interested in making healthcare better. How can we do things more effectively? That's what I was curious to know."

Listening to Alyce's recollections of this turning point in her life, I recognized something that I heard repeatedly in my conversations with unretired people:

There was an element of their work that instinctively fascinated them and provided a sense of direction that pulled them forward.

Moreover, as we'll see throughout this book, discovering and building on such a fascination was *the* decisive factor that, later in life, led them to reject the notion of retirement.

A FASCINATION WITH CHANGE

What fascinated Alyce, as she entered her 50s, was the prospect of changing the future of nursing care, and over the next decade she dedicated herself to this.

After divorcing the husband whom she felt might stand in her way, she embarked on a steep learning curve.

After my divorce, and receiving full custody of my children, I got my B.A. and master's degree in nursing. It was not a good experience. I couldn't figure out how I could make it with four children on my own, because nurses didn't make good money then.

But there comes a time when you have to figure out how to just do it. So, I continued to work full time and went for my PhD. I was always determined. My mother was convinced that if I hadn't wanted to be so educated, I would still be married. But I wanted my doctorate and I wanted to do research.

The purpose of the research she envisioned was to study what was working well in current nursing practice and what was ineffective or potentially harmful to patients.

To accomplish this, she first moved her family to a hospital in Oregon, then cross-country to the veteran's administration hospital in Portland, Maine, where she took on the newly established position of lead efficiency researcher and Associate Chief of Nursing Education.

Almost all of our research projects were related to bedside nursing, or the care provided by a health-care team. While patients are in the hospital, it's the nurses who take care of them, who deal with their pain, who deal with their nausea, who deal with their falls.

Our studies were sometimes about drugs, nutritional issues or mobility issues. Nurses would come to me with ideas. They were interested in trying this or that. And we would develop a randomized study around how to make a better outcome.

Today, this approach to fostering improvements in nursing, and in healthcare in general, is universally called "evidence-based practice." However, in the 1990s, when Alyce was experimenting with this methodology on the front lines of medicine, it was a truly revolutionary concept.

"For so long," she told me, "nursing had always been, you know, you do what the doctor tells you to do."

But when Alyce entered her early 60s, as a pioneer in her field, it was *she* who was telling doctors, pharmacists, dieticians, her nurse colleagues and hospital administrators how to continuously advance patient safety and medical outcomes.

And they weren't only listening but starting to pay her handsomely for her guidance.

Leaving the womb of employment, she launched her own independent consulting firm, named EVP Concepts (evidence-based practice), where she designed and conducted patient care research for hospital clients, while delivering workshops and lectures across the United States.

In her late 60s, she was named a Fulbright Specialist, a coveted honor among professionals and academics, and began traveling to parts of the Mideast, Asia, South America and Africa to share her expertise.

By age 80, when I visited with her, Alyce's pace had slowed slightly, not because of a lack of energy or commitment, but due to restrictions on international travel and in-person meetings in the wake of the coronavirus pandemic.

And her schedule was somewhat less hectic than before—that is, unless you counted her contract with the American Nursing Association to monitor improvements in nursing care nationwide; her time spent helping to run the healthcare system in Bozeman, Montana, where she lived; or her position as a high school, college and professional level track and field official, a sideline she had cherished over the previous 30 years.

As we wrapped up our visit, I asked Alyce, who was about to leave for a month in Africa, how she felt about being eight decades old, having 10 grandchildren and working 15 or more years beyond the age when many, if not most people, had thrown in the towel.

She responded:

I've never thought about getting old and I tease my kids because they are now all AARP eligible. At their age, now in their 50s, I felt like I was just getting started.

I'm still fascinated today by the work I do. And I think because I've stayed engaged, especially internationally, it's kept me always learning. My mind needs to always be learning. And, as a nurse, I think that's probably impacted my health, too, because I don't sit around and feel sorry for myself because I'm old.

So maybe with me as a model, my kids will think about not retiring, too.

Then, on saying our goodbyes, she turned the tables and asked if I could offer her a prescription: "What would I do," she hypothesized, "if I retired and wasn't doing these things that I do? What would I do with my time?"

I had to admit, I didn't have a clue.

CHAPTER THREE

An Unretirement Plan

To this point, you've read accounts of two highly effective professionals, radiologist Jim Demartini and research psychologist Rob Pascale, who miserably flunked retirement.

But change the names, the circumstances and the professions, and the underlying storyline merits continued exploration because it points the way to a seemingly counterintuitive realization:

The more successful you have been in your career, especially financially, the more likely you are to feel like a failure in retirement.

Let's see how this played out in the life of one highly innovative and accomplished entrepreneur.

HERE COMES THE SUN

When Robert Delamontagne retired at age 63, he thought the future looked bright.

Detail-oriented as always, he crunched the numbers in the back of his mind and concluded that he still had many excellent years ahead of him.

"I simply subtracted my age from the average life expectancy of an adult male, which is approximately 80 years," he recalled. "But I knew that I had a better chance of living longer, since both my parents lived into their 90s."

He felt blessed with financial security, good health and a loving family.

"All I needed was a little danger to keep it interesting," he told me. "So, I went out and bought myself a late model Porsche to feel the wind in my hair and sun on my face."

The wealth Robert had accumulated was hard earned and significant.

With a background in instructional design, in his late 30s, he had put the first technology-based educational system on a small computer and started his own company, EduNeering Inc., to further develop and take this breakthrough invention to the marketplace.

"It was extraordinarily difficult, like pushing a rock up a mountainside," he explained, "because no major corporation had ever seen education on a personal computer and I had to put 100% of my effort and energy into launching the business."

But after several years, his efforts started to pay off, and he soon began to reap the fruits of his success.

I liked winning, I liked making money, I liked the chase and the adventure of being in business and meeting people and having teams around me. A lot of venture capitalists invested in the business, and I loved the attention, the exposure, the accolades, and the respect of people when they knew me and were around me.

When Robert eventually sold his company to the education giant, Kaplan Incorporated, he expected these good vibrations to continue resonating throughout his retirement years.

Within a matter of a few months, however, to his surprise and consternation, the music stopped.

Nothing interested me. I didn't want to go anywhere or do anything because I'd already been there and done practically everything that I thought mattered to me.

I got involved in every aspect of running the house, which previously had been my wife's domain. You can imagine how well that went over.

I discovered that I didn't like fixing things and got
no pleasure from doing yard work.
    It was like living in a self-imposed dead zone.

Initially, Robert blamed his "dead zone" existence on two things: first, he felt that during his gangbuster business years he had unwittingly succumbed to what he termed an "achievement addiction." Second, he had been unaware, he said, that for high achievers like him, adapting to a retirement status could feel like an extended drug withdrawal.

But, on further reflection, and while writing a memoir about his experience, he came to realize that he should have anticipated how things would play out.

In his self-published book, *The Retiring Mind*, Robert wrote: "You slam a hard-charging personality type into an unplanned downsized retirement life, and you won't see stress like this unless you invested your retirement money with Bernie Madoff."

During our visit, Robert recounted a phone call that might have served to turn things around:

It had been well over a year since I had retired, and
my discomfort level did not seem to be improving. I
spoke with a good friend who was a clinical psychol-
ogist in Atlanta. He had recently lost his wife to

cancer, and we had spoken a few times in the previous months about our life-changing events.

My psychologist friend said: "Why don't you think about those things that you have done in the past that were successful and that gave you pleasure? This should give you some direction as to what you should be doing."

Sadly, however, some 15 years after that phone call, Robert acknowledged, at age 79, that he had never put his friend's advice into action. "Mentally and emotionally, nothing attracted me," he told me.

And now, after a battle with colon cancer, his energy was depleted, and he was, understandably, concerned about the time he had left while still regretting the missed opportunities of the past.

First of all I think I would have spent more time cultivating things that I enjoyed doing before I retired. I would have created an alternative reality for myself. I would have wanted to be an achiever. Or had the sense of achieving. I would not have been obsessed about it, but I would have wanted to be good at it.

In retrospect, the unfortunate bottom line for Robert, was that while he may initially have had the makings of a *retirement plan*, when things didn't work out as he had hoped:

He did not have, had not thought through, and had not pursued a successful "unretirement plan."

BUILDING BLOCKS OF SUCCESSFUL UNRETIREMENT

Clearly, for a highly effective professional like Robert, the glide path to happily ever after, rather than full-stop retirement, would have involved further cultivating his inherent fascination with business, reclaiming his joy of achievement and an additional element that he described this way: "I think what I would really love to do at this stage of life is help other people. That would mean a lot to me."

Indeed, for all the successfully unretired people whom I studied and spoke with while researching this book, the drive to help others, commonly called "generativity," served as one of the three essential building blocks of a joyful and fulfilling future.

While at first glance these concepts may seem abstract, they become relatively simple to grasp when placed in the context of real life.

A RETIREMENT AVERTED

Human resources executive Susan Nolingberg had recently celebrated her 60th birthday when the independent Texas oil company where she had worked for a quarter century, Burlington Resources, was purchased by energy giant ConocoPhillips, and her job disappeared.

When we met a decade later, she told me that affording full-stop retirement would not have been a problem, and she had given it some serious thought...for about a minute.

> *I had a nice severance. I could have just done nothing, but it would not have been very personally rewarding to me. I don't need to work, that's not why I'm working, but I've been able to live a very nice lifestyle with the additional income coming in. I'm 70 now and I've done some amazing things in the past 10 years that I wouldn't have experienced if I'd just hung it up.*

Everyone's definition of "amazing things," can significantly differ, of course.

In Susan's case, it was her abiding fascination with the development of highly complex executive compensation plans—the kind of work she'd first fallen in love with early in her career.

Fascination is the Foundation of Successful Unretirement

Through the compensation consulting practice that Susan launched after losing her job, she found herself involved with a much more diverse set of challenges, or "puzzles" as she called them, than she had ever previously grappled with.

> *In my work now I do a lot of things for a lot of different people. It could be anything—from a huge company to a start-up that needs a compensation structure. And what really excites me is the intellectual stimulation of all of this.*
>
> *I've got a client now that's a private company that's partly owned by Qatar Energy in the Middle East. And they have different ways of thinking about compensation plans than we do here in the U.S. So, I'm dealing with differing international cultures, differing corporate cultures and very different kinds of people.*
>
> *And it's really intense—just the way I like things.*

The experience of intensity that Susan mentioned is what sports and performance psychologists commonly refer to as being "in flow" or "in the zone."

And while flow is not frequently associated with designing corporate compensation plans, it can be triggered by any form of purposeful work into which we fully invest our talents, skills and energy.

So it stands to reason that Susan would experience its intensity while working on her compensation projects, because flow is commonly generated when we put our personal fascinations into action.

Flow is the Next Natural Building Block of Successful Unretirement

Mihaly Csikszentmihalyi (pronounced cheek-sent-me-high), the prolific performance researcher and psychologist who first discovered and named the flow phenomenon, considered it to be the highest level of human happiness, and explained its occurrence this way:

> [Contrary to what we usually believe... the best moments in our lives are not the passive, receptive, relaxing times. The best moments usually occur when a person's body or mind is stretched to its limits in a voluntary effort to accomplish something difficult and worthwhile.]

This is why engaging in challenges that stretch our minds and abilities, rather than pursuing less-demanding activities, is such an important building block of a successful unretirement plan.

After all, if doing work that fascinates us produces the highest level of happiness along with extra income, why not pursue it?

Among the leading symptoms of flow, some of which you may have personally experienced, are an experience of total immersion, lack of worry, sense of joyful mastery and the production of better-than-anticipated results in a state of being in which we don't notice the passage of time.

When I asked Susan whether she'd experienced manifestations of flow similar to these when working, she offered up a recent example.

> Just last week I was up until 2:30 a.m. a couple of nights in a row. That's one of my crazy work habits. But it doesn't bother me to be up working at all hours to get a project done. It's like a challenge, a puzzle to put the pieces together, and when it all fits together it's absolutely magical.

Concentrating on complex mathematical calculations through the night, not feeling fatigued and finding the results "magical" are certain signs that Susan's work gave rise to the flow experience.

Generativity is the Ultimate Building Block of Successful Unretirement

Prior to launching her consulting business, Susan seriously considered earning a degree and starting a new career in social work as a way of expressing her growing internal desire to be of assistance to others.

But when calls started coming in from younger executives seeking her compensation expertise, she discovered an outlet for this impulse without having to switch career tracks.

The social worker inside of me wants to help people, so this satisfies that need. I can go in when a client needs help, can get the project done and they're happy, and then I move onto the next project. My clients are very appreciative to have someone like me with the kind of knowledge and experience that can help them and their companies, and that's a great feeling.

Susan's special sense of satisfaction derived from what Harvard psychologist Erik Erikson, in the 1950s, labeled *generativity*, an innate human impulse to contribute or "pay it forward" to future generations.

[While studying the stages of adult development, Erikson contended that finding a way to express this drive was a crucial challenge in life's second half, which, if not adequately met, could lead to personal stagnation and emotional despair.]

In the years since his passing, high-level psychosocial research has, in fact, borne out Erickson's theory, establishing a direct association between generative behavior, stronger cognitive functioning, and lower levels of depression than is the norm in our 60s and beyond.

Simply put, doing work that pays it forward to the next generation has been shown in concrete terms to be a vital aspect of a successful unretirement plan.

Fascination, Flow and Generativity—rather than retiring, these are the building blocks with which Susan Nolingberg structured her life beginning in her early 60s. And they are the bedrock elements you will consistently see in the lives and extended careers of successfully unretired people in the pages to come.

You will also read a wide variety of declarations similar to Susan's when she told me:

I cannot imagine myself playing mahjong or pickleball every day. Unless my life were to change drastically, I will never quit working. It might not be what I'm doing now, but it will be something.

As we concluded our conversation, I asked Susan to assess—from her perspective as a human resources executive working with a range of individuals and companies—the current employment market for older workers.

> *I've seen it firsthand and right now I'm shocked by the number of businesses that are suffering because they can't get workers. There are just so many opportunities out there to serve and give and get paid for it, I don't know why people would think they have to retire. I don't know anyone who wants to work at this age who's not working. It varies with the industry, of course, and the moment in time, but overall, that's what I see.*

In the next chapter we'll visit an organization, one of the world's best-known, that sees things in much the same way.

CHAPTER FOUR

Miracle in the Cornfields

Heading southeast on U.S. route 52 out of Minneapolis, you soon find yourself surrounded by endless acres of soybeans, corn and wheat, dotted by exits to small towns with colorful names like Goodhue and Wanamingo, and billboards for local merchants like Corcoran Taxidermy, which proudly advertises: *"You Kill 'Em, We Fill 'Em!"*

Some 70 miles into this quiet, pastoral landscape, a small city skyline appears.

Leaving the highway and navigating toward its center, you skirt blocks of modest homes with cozy front porches, low-rise apartment buildings, and residential hotels mixed with towering edifices, some of them historic landmarks, others sleek and sparkling new.

Scattered within these structures are the offices, clinics and laboratories of 450 of the world's most accomplished medical doctors and researchers, all over age 65, and all passionately unretired.

This is Rochester, Minnesota, home of the famous Mayo Clinic, perennially ranked the number one medical center in the world.

Little known beyond Mayo's campus is the fact that its unretirees make up 10% of the total physician workforce, in which they are held, by administrators, younger colleagues and medical students, in high esteem.

"We're retaining their knowledge and experience within our walls," Dr. Chet Rihal, a member of Mayo's board of trustees, told me during my visit.

"We get people from all over the globe with serious and complex diseases, diagnostic dilemmas, and not everything can be solved with technology. It takes a high level of judgment, so the more experienced people we have around, the better for our patients. Secondly, we've got the largest graduate medical school in the country, and having good teachers and mentors is extremely important."

Despite brutal winters, long hours and fixed salary compensation that can be tens or even hundreds of thousands of dollars less than the income they might earn elsewhere, Mayo physicians remain on the job because of the special nature of the place—an island of advanced technology, high intellect and multispecialty teamwork in the midst of farmland along the banks of Minnesota's rambling Zumbro River.

Each year more than a million patients arrive here from every U.S. state and more than 150 nations.

And no wonder, given Mayo's history of medical innovations that include performing the first heart-lung-liver transplant, doing the first computerized brain surgery in the U.S., inventing the heart-lung bypass machine for open heart surgery, discovering cortisone to treat asthma, introducing the first CT scanner in North America and designing the first post-operative recovery room.

Among the many hundreds of celebrities, dignitaries and world leaders who have flown into Rochester's tiny airport are Billy Graham, Muhammad Ali, Ernest Hemingway, Johnny Cash, presidents Ronald Reagan and George H.W. Bush, and the Dalai Lama, who was treated here for cancer, and views the juxtaposition of nurture and nature as integral to Mayo's uniqueness.

Appearing in a PBS documentary about Mayo, he explained to filmmaker Ken Burns:

Sometimes I feel like big city looks like big machine. Their daily life without much thought of human feeling. I prefer people in rural area. Farmers you see more closer relation with nature. Farm area, rural area, more sense of community. The last nine, ten years annually, I come my medical checkup here. And many doctors I consider my old friends.

THE MAYO WAY

Friends are easy to come by at Mayo, and not just for VIPs.

In contrast to many healthcare environments, close doctor-patient relationships are part of the prescription for healing or, as they call it here, the "Mayo Way," in which the guiding principle is *"the needs of the patient come first."*

At the ground level what this requires is having doctors on staff who genuinely enjoy their work and spending time with patients—another exception to the get-em-in, get-em-out reality in much of American medical care today.

"I love what I do and I think I can speak for many Mayo physicians—there's nothing else I'd rather be doing," Dr. Rihal told me. "I've seen everything in terms of the technical aspects of medicine and it sounds a little corny, but what I'm finding is the more experienced and older I get the more rewarding I find my work."

THE RISKS OF RETIREMENT

I was especially interested in meeting with Chet Rihal because he held dual roles—he was a 28-year veteran and former chairman of Mayo's cardiovascular medicine department.

At the same time, he headed up the personnel committee—the place where decisions were made about training and hiring young physicians, and whether to retain them as they get older.

Of the 450 M.D.s over age 65 who work at Mayo, a good number are in their 70s, several are in their 80s and, at last count, one is still doctoring at age 90.

Before discussing these colleagues with him, and Mayo's policies regarding them, I thought it would be interesting to know Chet's personal plans for the future and how he felt, as one of America's leading heart doctors, about the concept of retirement.

I'm 61, so I'm at that age where I'm just now starting to think: "Gosh, I'm probably not going to work another 20 years. Am I going to work another 10 years? Probably."

I think 65 for most people is probably too early to hang it up because life expectancy is much longer today, and health and cognitive function is maintained for many people. As long as your mental faculties are sharp and you're enjoying it, I see no reason why people should hang it up.]

As a cardiologist I've worked with many retirees. Within six months they have these feelings of isolation and then loneliness, and depression can be a risk. So it's really important to have something to find purpose and meaning in. Those who do, tend to do better, physically and emotionally, than those who do not.

A HISTORY OF UNRETIREMENT

Working late in life was infused early into the Mayo Clinic's DNA.

Dr. William Worrall Mayo, the son of an English carpenter, came to America in the 1840s and earned degrees at Indiana Medical College and the University of Missouri, during an era in which few physicians had a formal education, and many were considered charlatans and quacks.

The small medical practice he subsequently established in rural Rochester was eventually passed on to his sons, Will and Charlie, following his retirement at age 70.

Today, this might not seem like a particularly advanced age, but consider: when he was born in 1819, life expectancy for men was just a smidge over 30 years.

"Dr. Will and Dr. Charlie," as his sons were affectionately known, grew up accompanying their father on house calls where he trained them to assist with patient exams and surgeries before they went on to earn their own medical degrees out of the area.

On returning to Rochester and establishing a joint practice, their innovations and surgical success rates began to attract patients from other states and countries—leading them to recruit other physicians with skills that were different but complementary to theirs.

Thus was born the then-unique multispecialty teamwork concept for which their practice, soon to be called the Mayo Clinic, became known.

Four decades and many thousands of procedures later, after the clinic they had launched amid cornfields had grown into a medical institution of global stature, Dr. Will unceremoniously put his scalpel down for the final time.

In her book, *The Doctors Mayo*, historian Helen Clapesattle relates the story this way:

> Dr. Will went to the clinic in a mood of deep depression. His secretary asked him what was the matter.
>
> 'I've just done my last operation. I want to stop while I'm still good. I don't want to go on like some

others I've seen, past my prime, doing surgery that younger, surer men ought to be doing.'

He never spoke of the matter, and never operated again—so little outward fuss did he make over a decision that must have been bitterly difficult for him.

Dr. Charlie's retirement from medicine came a year and a half later, suddenly and unexpectedly, as the result of a retinal hemorrhage that occurred one morning while he was operating.

Although leaving their surgical duties behind, they weren't done yet—Dr. Charlie continued leading the clinic's board of governors until his resignation at age 67, while Dr. Will finally stepped down at age 71.

Born in the 1860s, the brothers had an expected life span of about 40 years, meaning each of them had worked roughly three decades beyond their statistically predicted date of death.

Setting a remarkable example, to say the least, for Mayo doctors yet to come.

MAYO'S UNRETIREMENT PLAN

For all the Mayo Clinic's historic achievements, things have not always worked out as hoped or planned.

Like many of his colleagues at Mayo, cancer surgeon Mark Truty was all too familiar with the pain of failure.

"Every physician here has a personal, private cemetery in the back of their minds," he said, "it's the graveyard of all their previous patients they failed."

Hence the decision to keep doctoring later in life, rather than retire, is a weightier choice than continuing to work in careers in which the stakes are not as high.

Moreover, medicine is a field in which burnout and depression are common, with suicide rates higher among physicians than in any other profession.

So it takes a unique breed of doctors to stay on the job into their late 60s and beyond, as well as organizational policies that support and encourage them to do so.

"If you had asked me in my 50s if I'd still be working at the pace I'm working, doing what I'm doing at age 70, I'd have said no way," Tom Habermann, a veteran lymphoma clinician and researcher told me. "But my work has stayed relevant, and it's stayed interesting, so there's a certain sense of satisfaction that keeps me here."

Along with having no mandatory retirement age, Mayo's leadership team has put several unretirement-friendly mechanisms into place.

One allows physicians to scale back their hours beginning at age 65 if they no longer want to work full-time. As long as they continue working at least half of their previous schedules, they retain full employee benefits, which can be a significant incentive to stay on.

Alternatively, should they change their minds after initially retiring, and there's a continuing need for their expertise, they can return to work as independent contractors.

THE COMPETENCY TEST

While as we've seen, doctoring can pose emotional risks to physicians, so too there are occasions when younger colleagues, and occasionally patients, may raise concerns about older physicians being up to the job.

"Some people will probably think I should have gone out to pasture years ago," said Ronald Petersen, age 77, Mayo's leading Alzheimer's disease expert, adding "hopefully they were kidding when they said that."

Maybe so, but in some careers that require critical skills like his, age limits are serious business: under federal law, airline pilots must retire by their mid-60s; in a number of states, judges are required to step down by age 70; federal firefighters and some law enforcement officers are subject to mandatory retirement as well.

At Mayo, nevertheless, there's a strong feeling among administrators that the issues of age and physician competency have been safely and effectively addressed.

When I asked Chet Rihal about this, he responded that superior performance was expected and continually monitored for all physicians, regardless of age or years on the job.

> *We do expect top performance and, as you know, we work in a seamless fashion here. We work as a group practice. With our shared medical records, which date back to the earliest days here at Mayo, each of us can see what everybody is doing. So if somebody is not performing well, our staff can tell.*
>
> *But still, let's take someone who's one of the best surgeons in the United States and then he or she falls down to a very good level. What if they go from a super-star level down to very excellent? Isn't that sufficient?*
>
> *The more experience you get, the more you build up your skills, knowledge and judgment. And as long as your mental faculties are sharp and you're enjoying it, why hang it up? And as we know, cognitive dysfunction can happen at any age.*

Even to a skeptical journalist like me, Chet had a valid point.

And as we wrapped up our conversation, he offered several more observations, strongly supporting the retention and unretirement of experienced, older physicians.

> *There's a physician shortage in this country and it's going to get worse—if even half of them hang it up,*

we're going to be in dire straits. So I think from a hospital perspective there's going to be a greater need to retain and even bring back some of our retirees who have 30 or 40 years of experience.

And if you just look at the demographics in our country, we're going to need people to keep working. There are not enough millennials and Gen Zs coming along to replace all of us boomers. So we're going to need people in every profession and field.

Another point well taken, both in the short and long term.

MAYO'S CLASSIC ROCK STARS

Because they appear to have weathered the years so well, the continuing performances of celebrated rock n' roll stars in their late 60s, 70s and beyond frequently make headlines.

The morning after a music festival in Tennessee, for instance, a local newspaper wrote that 74-year-old singer-songwriter Stevie Nicks: "showed she still has what it takes to captivate a crowd...many not even born when Nicks was at the height of her career with Fleetwood Mac."

In 2023, *People* magazine reported that Ringo Starr, still drumming new tunes and touring with his All Starr Band at age 83, said: "Nothing makes me feel old. In my head, I'm 27."

But you don't hear much outside Rochester, Minnesota, about the older medical rock stars who live and work here, and whose achievements will continue to impact people's lives in a way that even the greatest song-writers and musicians cannot.

As mentioned before, many previously untried but now standard medical methods have been devised at Mayo: the first clinical trials of insulin were conducted here, the first tracer to detect invisible prostate cancers was invented, major advances in immunology were developed, and the list continues to grow each day.

This is the nature of the frontier on which Mayo's 450 unretirees have worked and continue their work today. And despite their heavy schedules, given my interest in their career longevity, I was able to arrange visits with several of them.

In our conversations, two aspects stood out in particular:

First, the key building blocks of successful unretire-ment that we explored in Chapter Three—Fascination, Flow and Generativity—were clearly present in their lives and work.

Second, they came across as energized, unwilling to rest on their laurels, and largely, if not entirely, uncon-scious of their age and the passage of time.

"Human beings are the most fascinating to me."

RUTH E. JOHNSON, M.D., AGE 70
SPECIALTY: INTERNAL MEDICINE

Born in Minneapolis in 1953, Ruth Johnson was a fifth-generation Minnesotan, whose Swedish ancestors flooded the state's small frontier towns in the 1800s, lured by inexpensive and fertile farmland.

It was hard to miss her signature Scandinavian features—blonde hair and sparkling eyes, behind which was a high level of personal commitment and professional curiosity.

"I'm a pretty high achiever," she told me. "I like to do well in everything that I do. Nobody gets to do this kind of stuff without being competitive, which runs through my family, but I think it's in the healthy range."

In high school, her favorite subjects were history and English, but her attention took "an incredibly different turn," as she put it, when Ruth's father fell ill, and she became one of his primary caregivers.

He inherited a kidney disease and became very sick. And he was hooked up on a hemodialysis machine so that he was able to live a year and a half on that, to keep him going.

He died when I was just 17 and the experience that I had watching him, the illness that he had, being in the hospital, completely changed my ideas about what I might do.

Within a few months before I started college, in August 1970, I thought I'd like to be a doctor and felt kind of a strong sense of a calling to do that. Never mind the fact that I had not taken chemistry, physics or trigonometry, because they didn't interest me. It was English that I loved!

At Augsberg University in Minneapolis, Ruth discovered a knack for subjects that she'd grown up disliking when, much to her surprise, science, chemistry and biology came more easily to her than expected.

She got straight As, and on graduation decided to apply to what was then the new Mayo Clinic medical school in Rochester, where she arrived to find that she was one of only nine women in her class of 40 students.

Upon earning her M.D. in 1978, Mayo offered her a residency along with continuing medical education, and that's when things began to get complicated—she couldn't figure out what kind of practitioner she wanted to be.

I had a little trouble with that. I clearly liked being a physician, but I was still very much tuned into relationships, intellectual pursuits, communication and all that.

So I got pulled in different directions. I struggled, and I did a year of psychiatry after med school, which I liked, and I think I could have been good at. I tried to do pathology for a while, but I eventually settled on internal medicine, which is what I practice now, and I'm very happy with.

FINDING HER FASCINATION & FLOW

For Ruth, it was in practicing internal medicine, or what's sometimes called "plain vanilla doctoring," that she first found the elements of *fascination and flow* that made her career a joy, she told me.

It's perfect because it has the sort of intellectual challenge, the diagnostician figuring stuff out. But probably the most joy I get is from relationships with people and patients. I love that kind of work.

How do you deal with a human being who has a disease or a problem or concern and really connect with them? I just enjoy that challenge. I like talking to people, I like finding out who they are, and I'm often more fascinated by that, than by the science itself.

Keep in mind, however, that the Mayo Clinic is where she worked—an environment in which enjoying one's job as a physician is certainly important, but above all, "the needs of the patient come first."

And it's for this reason that Ruth Johnson's passion for effective patient communication proved to be more than only salient over time—it became crucial.

What the American Medical Association calls medical non-adherence—failing to follow a doctor's guidance—has become one of the greatest challenges in modern healthcare.

According to the AMA, fear of side effects, the cost of medications and misunderstanding of doctors frequently lead patients to skip their prescriptions, resulting in potentially severe consequences, especially for those with chronic diseases.

As a result, Ruth Johnson's office visits became known as a clinical laboratory in patient care, a place where what she enjoyed doing most—the way she personally found flow—could impact the course of lives.

What's crucial is that I understand human beings—what motivates them, how we translate what we recommend for their health into things that help them understand their situation and motivate them to do this or that.

I have patients across the whole spectrum of intellect and sophistication, and I need to find ways to connect and communicate with them. Human beings are the most fascinating to me. Their psyche is part of the physical body, and that's what I need to connect with.

Ruth's work in this area positioned her on the leading edge of a new science called "motivational interviewing," in which experimentation with the most effective ways to connect with patients is central to the process.

When I talk to men, for instance, sometimes I can connect with them on things like golf. I need to communicate with them in ways that help them lose weight, or deal with high blood pressure, diabetes, or heart disease or high cholesterol.

Yes, you can use medications, but a lot of it is lifestyle— they need to lose weight, they need to get active. How do you do that? How do you get people to do what they need to do?

They've got to trust you and know that you know what you're doing, and that you have their best interest in mind. You need to find ways to connect with them to help them figure out their own situations and how they can make the changes they need to make.

EXPRESSING HER GENERATIVITY

Each pound a patient loses, each needed medicine they take, every question she effectively answers, is how Ruth has measured what she's accomplished in her long career and unretirement years.

And it's her sense of *generativity,* of contribution to her patients and profession, that has energized and motivated her to keep moving forward even if, at age 70, her body clock sometimes tells her to slow down.

> *I really enjoy what I'm doing. I feel like it's valuable, it's helping people, and you can't beat that, really. There are days when I don't get much sleep because I'm constantly running around, but I can still handle that. I still have a lot of physical stamina, which is probably genetic.*
>
> *But as long as I feel that we're doing the right thing by patients, that the needs of the patients come first, I feel like I can use the wisdom that I've gotten here over the years, along with new medical knowledge, to continue to work at full speed.*

**"I am concerned about full-stop retirement.
I'm not fearing it but at the same time
it'll be a difficult transition."**

RONALD C. PETERSEN, M.D. PH.D., AGE 77
SPECIALTY: ALZHEIMER'S DISEASE

As director of the Mayo Clinic Alzheimer's Disease Research Center and the Mayo Clinic Study of Aging, Dr. Ron Petersen had a unique technical perspective on the challenges of growing older.

On a personal level, still working at age 77, he had managed to avoid the well-documented losses that career professionals notoriously face when they call it quits.

The losses that the retirement research warns about— personal identity, purpose, social connections and meaning.

Ron's goal had been to steer clear of losing these as long as possible.

I have an older brother who is retired and he asked me when I was gonna retire. And I said: "Well, I dunno, probably pretty soon, but I'm still enjoying my work. And if I stop working a lot of that will stop, too." And my brother said: "Well, you're probably not going to retire, then." And I said: "Whaddya mean?" And he said: "Well, it's not a job, it's your life."

For me, it's a combination of, I enjoy doing it, I'm socially reinforced by other people for doing it, and I feel that I may be contributing to something. Also, I believe that staying intellectually active is good for the brain, maybe good for the body in general.

Ron's work had been at the center of his life for more than five decades. He was barely out of college, in fact, when he first found himself mesmerized by a puzzle:

Why do some people remember, why do some forget, and in either case, what's going on inside their brains?

It was a stroke of luck that first brought him face-to-face with this question—a set of circumstances that may have also saved his life.

In 1968, the year Ron received his undergraduate degree, nearly 17,000 U.S. troops were killed in Vietnam, and tens of thousands of men his age, from all over the country, were being drafted and shipped to the front lines each day.

Ron fully expected to be next in line. He recalled: "We had pre-induction physicals before we graduated because we were all going to be heading over there, sure as shooting."

Fortunately, things didn't turn out that way.

Instead, he was offered a full-time job by a company where he had worked during summers and his senior year,

Honeywell Incorporated, which was then doing psychological research for the Defense Department.

The offer included what was called a "critical skills" draft deferment—a deal that he, understandably, could not refuse.

"They had psychologists and physiologists doing interesting kinds of work in what were called human factors," he said, "and they also let me start graduate school, which kept me out of the draft for at least another year."

The Vietnam conflict wound down while he was attending graduate courses at the University of Minnesota, where his interest in what would become known as cognitive neuroscience—the biology of brain function—further escalated.

After earning his PhD, he went on to medical school, an internship at Stanford and a neurology residency at the Mayo Clinic, where he had a chance to focus on the puzzle that continued to fascinate him—now, in a highly-scientific environment.

As I gravitated toward medicine and the brain, my interest became what elements inside the brain allow people to remember well. What is it about the neurotransmitters, the chemicals in the brain, when problems develop and interfere with that? And then, hopefully, what we might do to reverse some of those disease processes.

In the examination rooms at Mayo, he repeatedly encountered the mother of all brain function puzzles—Alzheimer's disease.

And a decade after he began working there, he was assigned to care for the most famous of all Alzheimer's patients to that point in time—former president Ronald Reagan.

From the time Reagan left office, shortly after his 78th birthday, he had visited Mayo annually for routine physical and psychological check-ups.

According to biographer Craig Shirley, Reagan "had passed each year with flying colors until the spring of 1994, five years after he left the White House, when doctors noted that he was slipping, seeing memory loss that was more than age appropriate."

Working with his colleagues at Mayo, Ron Petersen was the first to diagnose Reagan with Alzheimer's and was the physician who called the Reagan home in Bel Air, California to report the news.

I talked to Mrs. Reagan and I talked to the president and both of them together. I think they took it in a matter-of-fact type of manner in which they dealt with many challenges in their life. I think while this was an important and devastating type of news for them, I think they took it in the sense that this is the next challenge, the next hurdle in their lives, so let's go forward from here.

Over the next decade, prior to Reagan's death in 2004 from Alzheimer's complications, a handful of new drugs became available that could target, and in some instances lessen, the memory and thinking disturbances that appear as the disease worsens.

But the underlying brain biology of Alzheimer's, and ways to potentially address it, remained a puzzle.

Until 2010, when Ron and fellow researchers began to identify the protein-based brain plaques and tangles that they suspected to be causing the disease.

Their research eventually led to accelerated federal approval in 2021, of aducanumab, the first drug designed to remove these plaques and thereby slow cognitive and functional decline in people with early Alzheimer's.

Several additional drugs that work similarly have since been approved; and while still not a cure, they constitute enormous clinical leaps from the days when young Ron Petersen first set out to solve his puzzle.

When we diagnose Alzheimer's disease these days, it's not just that you've got gradual forgetfulness over the last five to six years and now it's affecting your

daily function. That's the way we made Alzhei-
mer's disease diagnoses 10 or 20 years ago.

Now I can look inside your brain with a scan
and see if your forgetfulness is due to the develop-
ment of these proteins, these amyloid proteins, that
cause the plaques and tangles of Alzheimer's disease.
And now we have drugs that can actually lower the
amount of these proteins in the blood and body and
brain and try to slow down the disease.

Now we can say: "Hey, I know what road you're
on, you know what road you're on, and now I think
we can do something about it."

Before Ron had to run off to another research meeting,
I raised the same question that he said his brother had
once asked him—when, if ever, did he plan to retire?
He responded:

I work around a lot of very bright young people here
who just blow me away in terms of their insights,
their intuitive grasp of what's going on in the brain,
where they see the field going in the future.

And it's just exciting to be around them and
I don't know if I lend any wisdom to them. But
hopefully, having been here on the research front
for 40 years, we've built an infrastructure that when
I walk away, nobody will miss me— because they

can use that and build upon it and expand it for
the next generation.

As I suspected might happen, he didn't directly answer my question.

And as I left the Mayo Campus, driving back out through the lakes and rolling hills of Minnesota, it struck me that most of Mayo's elders had never taken the time to proactively map out their unretirement plans.

Rather, as if by instinct, they had arrived at a formula that worked for them.

At its core, it was that which Sigmund Freud, who worked until the time of his death, described more than a century ago:

"Love and work...work and love, that's all there is.
Love and work are the cornerstones of our humanness."

For the unretirees at the Mayo Clinic, this was a prescription that has no expiration date.

CHAPTER FIVE

A Life with No Name

On the eve of the year 2000, executives at the American Association of Retired Persons knew they had a problem.

Leading edge baby boomers—those born in the late 1940s—were reaching their 50th birthdays and automatically receiving AARP membership cards in the mail.

"Dear friend," read the greeting, "the enclosed AARP card has never been more valuable to you than it is today. As a matter of fact, life is just beginning at age 50."

For many, AARP's version of life was one they hated thinking about—they didn't want to be reminded that they were growing older, didn't want to join a club that included their parents, and had no desire to be associated with an organization whose initials might as well be RIP.

Horace Deets, then AARP's executive director, had seen signs of this coming years earlier, he told me.

My dad used to say when I first went to work for AARP: "Don't send me that membership card." And I would say: "Why's that?" He would say: "Because I'm not ready to retire. I've noticed that a lot of my friends have retired, and a few years later I'm going to their funerals. I don't give a damn what the coroner thinks, I think they died of boredom."

But now, Horace and his colleagues were hearing ominous murmurs from the largest and most highly educated generation in American history, which was solidly immersed in its prime earning years, and telling pollsters that they viewed retirement as a "maybe never" proposition.

So indeed, the American Association of Retired Persons had a puzzle to solve, as an organization that thrived on a growing membership base.

What do you call this new emerging stage of life?

After studying the question intently, in February of 1999 the association went public with its solution: "The American Association of Retired Persons officially changes its name to AARP, in recognition of the fact that many members continue to work full or part time."

Simply put, they punted—and the reaction was swift and merciless.

"Their solution to the problem made it worse," marketing expert James R. Rosenfield told the news media. Besides, he said: "AARP is the world's worst acronym, it sounds like a dog barking, like aarp, aarp!"

"They think they're going to camouflage themselves and get away from an inappropriate name," said Steve Rivkin, president of a New Jersey marketing firm. "It should have been a new name with a new identity."

But they didn't have a new name to offer up and, as a result, their challenge got even worse.

In early 2001, attempting another way to convert unretired baby boomers into fans, AARP launched a snazzy new magazine called *My Generation* that was sent to younger audiences in place of *Modern Maturity*, which continued being sent to the retired crowd.

The premier issue of the new publication featured a cover story on actor Ed Harris, then age 51, along with articles about tech gadgets, financial planning and camps that provided trapeze lessons.

Within two years this venture went bust as well, and both of AARP's magazines were folded into a single new offering simply titled: "*AARP: The Magazine.*"

In other words, they punted again.

The *New York Times* summed up the situation: "Of all the challenges that AARP faces, perhaps the greatest is keeping a cohesive purpose and sense of direction with a membership that is split by an age gap and a sense of identity. The organization may be poised to achieve explosive growth, but it also has to figure out how to appeal to people who are 50 to 65 and still working."

The folks at AARP were hardly the only ones struggling to figure this out.

The very nature of life's second half was transforming—some were onboard, some were mightily resisting the inevitability of change, and only a rare few had an inkling of how to keep up.

One was Mitch Anthony.

THE FINANCIAL PHILOSOPHER

As a boy, Mitch experienced a trauma that helped to chart the course of his life and career.

"My first recollection is that my grandfather was a successful salesman," he told me. "Then he retired and was dead in six months. He literally had no reason to get up in the morning."

For Mitch, the incident morphed into a personal philosophy:

I think boredom's a big deal and I don't think it gets enough underscoring. I meet people all the time on the golf course and I ask them: "Are you retired?" And they say: "Yeah, well I retired for a year and I couldn't take it anymore and I had to do something." They felt useless and saw themselves slipping into bad habits—that's my personal theory.

In the early 2000s, as America's retirement industry, including AARP, began grappling with the country's dramatically changing demographics and attitudes, Mitch turned his theory into a crusade.

He wrote a book calling for a sea change in the national conversation about getting older, from one that centered on retirement savings and leisure, to one that included continuing work and the financial benefits this could offer.

["Money can fund purpose," he wrote, "but it cannot create purpose. There needs to be a balance," he proposed, "between vacation and vocation."]

At first, he didn't get far with this approach because few people knew who Mitch Anthony was.

Then came his big break.

After spending the early years of his career leading programs in secondary schools, "the door opened in the financial services industry," as he put it, and a new horizon appeared.

I'd always been intrigued by this realm because the entire financial services industry was literally built around the proposition of retirement. I started writing about my ideas, and I was very fortunate that a mutual fund company came along and said: "We want to license these ideas from you."

In his new role as a fully-vested financial philosopher, Mitch not only wrote about his ideas, but also sought opportunities to present them directly to a highly influential crowd—financial advisors and planners whose clients included current and would-be retirees.

His premise was that the financial advisors, their industry, and the clients they served would all benefit greatly by having financial plans that recognized that many 50 to 65-year-olds no longer fashioned themselves as retirees in waiting, but instead planned to keep working and generating income as long as they could.

The thing I was trying to get planners to do was to stop assuming that everybody's gonna exit the workforce at 65 and stop plugging that into the financial plans they put together for their clients.
[The whole path of life was evolving. It used to be a three-step path: you learned, you earned, and then you adjourned. That was once the path for everybody, but not anymore.]

Master salesman and scribe that he was, Mitch proposed a way to capture the essence of America's new emerging stage of life. Throwing down the gauntlet before those who had failed to successfully characterize it so far, he labeled it:

THE NEW RETIREMENTALITY

In a speech to the Financial Planning Association of America, Mitch spelled out his concept this way:

> *W-O-R-K is no longer a four-letter word. We are living in an age of renaissance regarding the place of work in our lives. We are beginning to fully understand the virtues and benefits of being engaged in productive and affirming pursuits.*
>
> *Unfortunately, for many workers entering their 60s, the drudgery of toiling in enervating careers has dulled this comprehension to the point that they are ready and willing to believe the mendacious mythology of the "play all day" Del Webb mirage in the desert.*
>
> *The question I would like to pose to the financial planning community is: Why not you? Why shouldn't you be the person starting a new conversation with clients regarding the investment of their intellect, experience and soul capital into our society? This is part of the retirement planning conversation of our present age.*

[*As planners, you have a unique opportunity to encourage your clients to live a life of balance between vacation and vocation. Therein lies the true oasis of retirement.*]

When I last spoke with Mitch, in the spring of 2023, he was 64 years old and had no plans, unsurprisingly, to ever retire. "I can't stand being bored," he said, "I would go insane."

I asked if he thought his "new retirementality" idea had stood the test of time.

It never blew up really big like I thought it might, but in the realm of financial services, they know about it. This year marks the 25th year that they've been paying me to use my ideas.

I saw a campaign from Merrill Lynch that was almost just word for word from my book, which was titled "The New Retirementality." So I think there's ample proof that people are thinking about that more than they were 20 years ago.

He's right—in his own unique way, Mitch began to transform and update the conversation about the new stage of life that did not yet have an official name.

NEXT UP: MARC FREEDMAN & FRIENDS

While Mitch Anthony was soldiering on as a lone ranger within his industry, a social visionary named Marc Freedman brought a team of experts and the deep pockets of some of the country's leading foundations to the challenge that Mitch had tackled.

With a background in the nonprofit sector, Marc had an ax to grind with the retirement industry and a unique perspective on what Americans should do once they left their primary careers behind.

In a series of books and well-placed articles, he glommed the financial services industry together with real estate developers and labeled them "inventors of the Golden Years," who, he contended, were hypnotizing people with visions of endless leisure in order to siphon off their pensions and social security payments.

Wrote Marc:

> The financial services companies' extensive marketing efforts succeeded in elevating the idea that retirement was not something to be feared or dreaded, but rather the opposite: a new version of the American dream. Soon the Golden Years lifestyle began to radiate throughout the country.
>
> Once communities like Del Webb's Sun City and its chief rival, Leisure World, emerged as emblems of retirement, a vast leisure sector

followed. In a relatively brief period, these interests transformed the ideal of retirement into one of endless vacation.

Throughout public presentations and media interviews, Marc painted a very different picture of the way people should invest their later years: they should work for or create nonprofit organizations that would provide them with "passion, purpose and a paycheck," while tackling some of society's biggest challenges.

He was a fervent believer in the notion that people in life's second half constituted a "deep repository of life experience" that could be leveraged for the greater good.

When we sat down together in his Berkeley, California, living room, Marc explained:

I think when people come to this stage of life they recognize that the years ahead are likely fewer than the years behind them. But they feel like the impact of these years could last quite a long time.

These people have both a lifetime of experience and a full chapter left to put that experience to use. So they can do more than leave a legacy. They can live one, and I think that could be the watchword for this generation.

Remember, for decades we heard that awful slogan: "I'm spending my children's inheritance?"

Well, I'd like to see all those bumper stickers plastered over with one that says: "I'm leaving my legacy and living it."

Simply writing and talking about this was not sufficient in Marc's view—something big needed to be done about it.

With an undergraduate degree and MBA from Yale, he had friends and connections in high places whom he enthusiastically recruited to help found a nonprofit called Civic Ventures, through which he raised funds from major philanthropies to launch a significant social movement.

REFRAMING RETIREMENT

On a trip to New York, Marc was introduced to a woman who would prove to be indispensable in his drive to replace retirement with the new "good works" stage of life he envisioned.

Ruth Wooden was well known on Madison Avenue, where America's major advertising and PR agencies had their headquarters. She had been executive VP and director of cause-related marketing at the global public relations firm, Porter Novelli, then moved on to be the first female president of the Advertising Council, the country's top producer of public service campaigns.

Then in her 50s, Ruth had grown a little nudgy in her job and, when she met Marc, was already pondering what to do next.

The nonprofit that Marc had started and the focus of his work, Ruth told me, seemed like a perfect match for her talents and experience.

> *I had done a lot of work on baby boomers as a marketing force and, as it turned out, I was a proverbial canary in the mine for baby boomers, having been born in 1946 myself.*
>
> *I had learned throughout my career that being such a canary in the mine gave you a kind of head start in being able to predict various trends and interests. I could tell what was going to be hot in a few years because it was something I was thinking about. It's not that I'm so insightful, it's just that it was all in the demographics.*

After joining the board of Marc's organization, Ruth helped to launch a series of in-depth studies into what her generation, the baby boomers, wanted to do with the rest of their lives.

> *We were hearing a lot of: "Oh my God, I don't want to play golf for 10 years," as people were beginning to get a sense of this new longevity and the likelihood*

that their lives were going to be a lot longer than previous generations.

[And now you had this kind of leading edge of the baby boom saying: "Geez, retirement isn't for me. I want to keep working. I don't want to work like I always did, but I want to work at something else."]

At some point during a board meeting, as Marc will tell you, I said: "It's not just a new stage of life we're looking at—it's a new stage of work." And that's when we got started thinking about how to put a name on this concept.

The name they crafted for their retirement-replacement concept was <u>Encore</u>, which subsequently became the name of their organization, the title of a new book by <u>Marc</u>, and the idea behind the social movement they intended to foment, which they called:

THE ENCORE SOCIETY

Together, they recruited key journalists and thought leaders to join the board of <u>Encore.org</u> and help spread the word. Among them were <u>Ellen Goodman,</u> a Pulitzer Prize-winning newspaper columnist, Suzanne Braun Levine, founding editor of Ms. Magazine, and Jim

Emerman, former chief operating officer of the American Society on Aging.

With this firepower behind them and funding from socially conscious organizations, including Atlantic Philanthropies and the John Templeton Foundation, they launched a variety of initiatives to encourage non-retirees to seek jobs in the nonprofit world or become social entrepreneurs in areas such as health care, education and environmental sustainability.

In the decade to follow, however, their Encore Society ran into economic roadblocks: the recession of 2008-9 devastated budgets in the social sector, stunting the progress of encore career seekers; nonprofits launched by encore entrepreneurs suffered when contribution streams dried up.

Speaking with Marc in 2012, I could sense that, while still hopeful, he was chastened by the rough seas he had encountered.

I feel like there's this great migration happening, yet the territory is uncharted and people are just now charting it. They're building the paths, the roads and the infrastructure to make it easier for so many more who are coming behind them.

But the road is rocky and there are lots of obstacles along the way, and I think it could be

discouraging for many people. It's not easy to be a
pioneer.

A decade later, Encore.org ceased to exist and was replaced by Marc and his associates with a new organization and focus.

Still, it was not a lost cause the way Marc saw it—for a while, at least, it gave a name, albeit with a not-for-profit focus, to the emerging stage of life that was increasingly supplanting retirement.

In the meantime, a more permanent, all-encompassing label for this new lifestyle was being quietly placed on the table.

AND THE WINNER IS...

With growing numbers of retirement-age knowledge executives and professionals continuing to work, returning to work or launching new businesses and careers, Chris Farrell, a well-respected analyst for NPR and American Public Media, wrote a semi-scholarly book that highlighted what economists were increasingly calling "a revolution in the making."

In his book, Farrell quoted a senior advisor to AARP as saying that "older workers are going to change the workforce as profoundly as women did."

Published in 2014, Farrell's title seemed to say it all: *Unretirement: How Baby Boomers are Changing the Way We Think About Work, Community, and the Good Life.*

UNRETIREMENT

Period, full stop.

That's what this new stage of life is, for the rapidly growing millions of Americans who can't see long-term golfing, gardening, cruising, boozing or sunning at the pool as the path to happily ever after.

Unretired is what to call them, and there's really no point adding anything more.

CHAPTER SIX

Examining the Unretired Brain

As I conducted interviews for this book, I couldn't stop wondering how the unretired professionals I had been meeting, especially those in their late 70s and beyond, could continue to work successfully at jobs that required such high-level analytical skills.

People like Dr. Ronald Petersen, age 77, who was still engaged in complex research on Alzheimer's disease at the Mayo Clinic; Louis Primavera, age 80, who continued to design and teach others how to leverage sophisticated market data; or Jeanette Hobson, also age 80, who remained a magnet for CEOs half her age in need of top-notch management consulting.

What exactly was going on with their mental longevity? Were they outliers? Freaks of nature? Or was there something about them that we are either unaware of or blind to?

After all, most of us have been led to believe that, as early as our 60s, we begin a downhill slide on which our cognitive and intellectual abilities inevitably decline; that the older we get, the more likely we are to need prescription drugs to maintain clarity of mind; or, at the very least, we'll require crossword puzzles or brain stimulation games to help us remember where we put our car keys.

But more than 15 years ago, while doing research for an earlier book, I discovered that neuroscience experts were beginning to find, through the use of new brain imaging technologies, that nearly everything they had always thought about lifelong mental potential was misleading and outdated.

Leading brain scientists and neuropsychiatrists were concluding that, contrary to earlier assumptions, the human brain did *not* necessarily wear down or out with time; that older brains are *not* naturally inferior to those of younger people, but rather organized differently.

To my mind, this was exciting and revolutionary information that I needed to share with my readers—but at the same time it felt somewhat scholarly and hard to fathom in the abstract.

Now here I was, in 2023, seeing for myself that the brains of some octogenarian professionals did not merely have the potential, but were actually performing at higher levels than the brains of counterparts many decades younger.

What did this suggest about the way we've traditionally designed our lives and careers—about our true capabilities in our 70s, 80s and beyond?

From my work in the management development field, I knew of a luminary whose life and writings shed bright light on the answers to these questions.

THE FATHER OF THE KNOWLEDGE ECONOMY

If there ever was an unretired brain worth examining, it would be that of Peter F. Drucker, known in the business world as the undisputed "founder of modern management."

Over a period of seven decades, from the 1930s until his death at age 96, Drucker authored hundreds of highly respected articles and more than 35 books that have sold tens of millions of copies in more than 30 languages and are still considered essential reading for leaders and managers worldwide.

What even his most ardent admirers may not know about Drucker is that *he wrote nearly two thirds of his books after age 65,* while also speaking and consulting widely, and teaching at Claremont Graduate University in California, where the Drucker School of Management was later established in his name.

Another fact of which some are unaware is that it was Drucker in the late 1950s who first coined the term "knowledge worker," predicting that highly trained and educated individuals—people who *think* for a living— would soon become the most valuable assets in any company or organization.

Within a few short years he was shown to be prophetic—with the availability of early information technologies in the 1970s, manual labor and manu-facturing began to give way to the new brain-based knowledge economy in which so many of us have spent our careers.

In his writings, Drucker underscored this as well: for yesteryear's manual workers who spent "forty years in the steel mill for instance, or the cab of a locomotive," as he put it, retirement was a natural and ultimately necessary stage of life.

Their bodies would be tired and they would be "quite happy," he explained, to spend their post-work years "doing nothing, playing golf, going fishing, engaging in some minor hobby and so on."

But people who earned a living with their minds— knowledge executives, professionals and workers—would be faced with an entirely different reality as they grew older.

Unless their brains were injured or malfunctioning due to disease, there would be no reason why they would ever wear down or out.

So should they choose to, they could apply their accumulated knowledge, experience and brainpower every day for the rest of their lives—they could possess and benefit from using, in other words, *unretired brains* with enormous capacity and unlimited potential.

There was only one hitch, Drucker warned: "If knowledge isn't challenged to grow, it disappears fast. It's infinitely more perishable than any other resource we have ever had."

State-of-the-art neuroscience has since shown Drucker to be prescient about this, as well, right down to the cellular level.

THE SPEED OF KNOWLEDGE

Until recently, it was widely accepted by scientists, and conveyed to the rest of us, that the human brain was only capable of growth and development during the early decades of life. After that, they believed, our brains became fixed machines, not unlike aging and increasingly fragile computers.

In the late 1980s, however, Michael Merzenich, a neuroscientist at the University of California–San Francisco, began to question this assumption and set out to determine if it was actually true.

What he found instead, first in experiments with monkeys and then humans, was that our brains are capable of absorbing new knowledge and developing new skills at every stage of life, from "cradle to grave" as he characterized it.

His discovery, which he labeled "brain plasticity," was a complete paradigm shift in the neuroscientific community, where he and his revelations were initially rejected with a snobbish harrumph.

Wrote Merzenich:

"My colleagues and I were subjected to very strong criticism by powerfully entrenched investigators. They held that the deficits recorded when a child entered school, for example, would have to be accepted as a fixed, largely inherited, reality. And that the physical brain from a young age onward had only one trajectory: downhill. For me, nothing could be further from the truth."

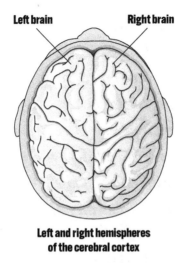

Left and right hemispheres of the cerebral cortex

Neuroscientist Michael Merzenich was the first to discover and document that the human brain remodels itself in response to learning and experience.

About a decade later, when I sat down to discuss this with him on a PBS Television special, Merzenich's findings had become universally accepted, and he spoke of them with an even deeper understanding than when he first arrived at them.

Below are some excerpts from our conversation:

Mark Walton: With regard to the long-term potential of the human mind, what word or words would you use to characterize this?

Dr. Merzenich: We're continuously plastic, we have the capacity to change to the end of our life. We have the capacity to be stronger, better, to have deeper understanding, to extend our capacities, to extend our abilities at any point in life. Of course, that same gift can contribute to our progressive demise because plasticity is a two-way process.

[*If you retreat, if you retire or withdraw from life, your capacities will slowly regress. And most people in older life have this fate. They substantially withdraw from life, or they allow their growing weaknesses to overwhelm them. And they become reduced in life, they become a kind of caricature, a more limited person as a consequence of this.*]

Mark Walton: *Tell me about the worldview in neuroscience before you discovered this and how you went about changing it.*

Dr. Merzenich: *The widely accepted view was that you were stuck with your genetics because you were stuck with a physical and functional brain that was established in a fixed and inalterable form. And that's just simply not true.*

What happened was that we began to do experiments in the mainstream of neuroscience, studies that were conducted in my laboratory and others, which showed that each time you acquire a skill or ability in older age, at any age in fact, the brain remodels itself.

We began to look, for example, at animals near the end of life, animals that were thought to be very limited in their ability. And we found that we could actually drive very substantial improvements in their brain performance. We found that, given the power of plasticity, their older brain could change almost like a brain in the prime of life.

And this carried us very rapidly to doing the equivalent kinds of studies in humans—documenting the same kinds of changes occurring in the brains of humans at any age.

A RETIRING MIND

As I grappled with what Merzenich had uncovered, part of my own brain flashed back to memories of my grandfather.

The son of immigrants from Romania, he spent his working years building one of America's first men's clothing chains, with retail stores on prime city real estate across the country. Visiting his home as a boy, I would watch him come downstairs each weekday morning, impeccably dressed, have a light breakfast while scanning the newspaper, then head for the train and his headquarters in Manhattan.

To my eyes, he was the very picture of a man with purpose.

Then, following his own company policy, he retired in his mid-60s, and soon became someone I no longer recognized.

Despite a circle of friends to golf and play cards with, travels abroad in luxury, and a bevy of grandkids to enjoy, he became pedantic, 'sweating the small stuff' of daily living and ruminating on people he thought had wronged him over the years.

As I grew older, I began to speculate on the reasons behind this, but had no basis for understanding what had happened in the mind of this man who was such an important part of my life.

Until neuroscientist Michael Merzenich laid it all out for me.

> *The brain slows down later in life in part because of the way the average person uses or, more importantly, does not use it.*
>
> *It runs a little like the performance peak of an athlete. You're at your peak roughly around your 30th birthday, and from that point forward you slowly slide backward. For instance, if you thought about it from the point of view of a professional athlete or a theoretical physicist, by your 40th*

birthday you're going to be struggling to still hang in there.

But what we now know is that you can slow down this regression as a function of how you use your brain. Most people are unaware of the fact that their performance capabilities are substantially under their control. They're unaware that their brain is in fact plastic, and so they accept the downhill slide and down they go.

On the other hand, there are individuals who don't move backward in a perceivable way until very near the end of life. And those are individuals that have found the magic ways, you could say, to maintain themselves, to maintain their capacities at a high level. When we change behavior, we change the brain, and that's the fundamental bottom line here.

My grandfather lived into his 90s in good physical health—I only wish he had known that he might have changed the quality of his final decades by changing what his brain was focused on.

MERZENICH'S PRESCRIPTION

Michael Merzenich's approach to the subject of retiring was simple and straightforward—don't even think about it.

Consider your brain a muscle, he said, and regardless of your age, push it to its fullest potential. And while Merzenich had personally invented brain development software that could slow cognitive decline, these were no substitutes, he asserted, for living a life that included a profession or work that regularly challenged and thereby continued to develop the brain.

The earlier we begin to understand and apply this knowledge, he told me, the better.

> *Mark Walton: Is the physical analogy something like marathon running? That is, you can start running marathons later in life, but you'd be better off to start young and continue running. And the same goes for continuing to exercise your brain, because while it isn't technically a muscle, it's analogous to one—is that correct?*
>
> *Dr. Merzenich: It is analogous to a muscle, Mark. And in a well-led life you would consider your brain fitness, your neurological abilities, and try to do what's necessary to sustain these as close to the*

*peak as possible at all times. And that's absolutely
possible. You know, what a gift it is that we have
the ability to keep ourselves at that high operational
level in our 70s, 80s or however long we live.*

When last I checked on him, Michael Merzenich
was, unsurprisingly, unretired at age 81—still lecturing
and writing about brain plasticity and working as Chief
Scientific Officer at Posit Science Corporation, the San
Francisco-based brain development software company
that he had co-founded in his late 50s.

THE WISDOM PARADOX

Over time, as I digested my conversation with Michael
Merzenich, what he had told me became increasingly
clear—if we continue to challenge our brains later in life,
the way we did in high school, college or grad school, they
will "remodel" themselves, as he put it, to absorb and use
knowledge as rapidly and efficiently as they did when we
were younger.

Still, as I continued my visits with unretired executives
and professionals, something else kept cropping up about
their cerebral abilities that intrigued me.

As a matter of course, I often asked unretirees what,
if any, changes they noticed in their daily work—did

they feel, for instance, less focused, less energetic or less creative, perhaps due to their age?

They commonly responded that they felt much the same way they had when they were younger except for one surprising development: they found that *their work actually came more easily to them* and that, in particular, they were now able to *jump more rapidly and accurately to conclusions* than they had earlier in their careers.

Seventy-year-old cancer researcher Tom Habermann, for example, said that he frequently met with highly trained young colleagues at the Mayo Clinic who brought him detailed patient laboratory and imaging reports accompanied by uncertainties about what to do next.

After reviewing their cases, Tom was able to rapidly identify the "needle in the haystack" of the extensive medical data they provided, and confidently point the way to the most effective course of treatment.

Why was he able to accomplish this—and what, if anything, did it have to do with the capabilities of his older, yet unretired brain?

MODULES OF EXPERIENCE

As I began to seek answers, I learned of Elkhonon Goldberg, a noted neuropsychologist in New York City who had a long history and unique expertise in this area.

On my trip to meet with him, I read into his book, *The Wisdom Paradox: How Your Mind Can Grow Stronger as Your Brain Grows Older,* which, based on the title alone, seemed to hold promising insights.

Goldberg, then age 65, was both a clinician and prolific researcher specializing in cognitive neuroscience—the link between brain activity and thought processes.

Early in his book, Goldberg pinpointed from personal experience what I had heard in my interviews with other unretired knowledge executives and professionals:

"Frequently, when I am faced with what would appear from the outside to be a challenging problem," he wrote, "the grinding mental computation is somehow circumvented and rendered, as if by magic, unnecessary. The solution comes effortlessly, seamlessly, seeming by itself."

As this was precisely what had prompted my visit with him, to begin our conversation, I asked for an explanation of this odd phenomenon and why it seemed to appear later in life.

This is the central paradox of the older brain, he asserted—while some mental processes, such as memory, may become more difficult, new strengths and abilities emerge.

Dr. Goldberg: And this is what people sometimes refer to as the illusive concept of wisdom. And the mere fact that we talk about wisdom and link it to aging implies that we all intuitively sense that there are certain aspects of our minds which actually improve as we grow older.

Mark Walton: Technically speaking, what's going on here? What makes wisdom, or whatever we call it, show up later in life?

Dr. Goldberg: In my work, I focus on a mechanism called pattern recognition. That is, as we go through life, we accumulate certain mental representations which enable us to acquire these abilities.

Simply living into old age alone does not guarantee anything. But those of us who have lived lives filled with cognitive challenges develop certain cognitive strategies which enable us to encounter seemingly novel problems as though they were familiar.

And this is a very powerful tool that our brain possesses, which clearly requires time to develop, and which enhances our cognition and protects us from the mental effects of aging.

Mark: I'm not a neuroscientist, so I'm not qualified to try to simplify what you're saying, but it sounds like what we're talking about here is the neuroscientific equivalent of experience.

Dr. Goldberg: Correct—there are modules of experience, not just any kind of experience, but certain kinds of experience which enable you to encounter a technically new situation, and immediately recognize the essential features in it which are familiar, and for which you have strategies to deal with it.

What Goldberg initially referred to as "pattern recognition," he also called "cognitive templates," a term that he and others in his field consider to be the foremost mechanism behind higher-order or "critical thinking" skills.

Concerning the development of these mental attributes as we age, Goldberg wrote in his book: "The first message is that those of us whose mental lives have been both vigorous and rigorous approach their advanced years with a mighty mental coat of armor. This armor, a mental autopilot of sorts, will serve them in good stead in the final decades of life."

Mark: In practical terms then, this seems to prove that no matter your field, experience seriously matters. That the brain of an older, experienced professional possesses strengths and assets that it lacked decades earlier, and that younger professionals do not yet have.

Dr. Goldberg: Absolutely, and that's precisely it. There are cognitive strategies which enable an older person to engage in all kinds of mental economies, to know how to deal with seemingly new situations as though they were familiar.

Think of any professional, like a physician encountering a patient they've never seen before. If they are experienced, it immediately resonates with some previous example of what treatments were helpful, so that is a great facilitator in their diagnostic approach. The same is true for an engineer, or for an architect who is designing a new object and draws on the vast experience of his or her previous challenges.

Mark: You and I were born within a few years of each other. We're both knowledge professionals, as are many of the people around us. Our generation will live longer on average than any population in *history that came before us. What should every-thing you've told me about our mental capacities mean to us, as individuals, and as a group?*

Dr. Goldberg: *Maybe we should be the first gener-ation who will refuse to retire, who will continue to strive to create until we drop and go to heaven. This is my plan—never retire. What would I do if I were to retire? We should strive to be creative and productive in any way we can, but basically refuse to accept this notion of retirement as a natural stage of life. I personally think that it's terribly unnatural.*

"New strengths that emerge later in life," Goldberg wrote, "may allow for the discharge of very high level professional and executive responsibilities and even world class feats of artistic and scientific creativity and states-manship. History is replete with examples of great creative genius and political genius reaching its peak only at the age of sixty, seventy, even eighty."

That's truly amazing, I thought, as I headed out onto West 57th Street near Goldberg's office in Manhattan. And now, after my conversations with him and Michael Merzenich, I understood why it was so.

FAMOUS UNRETIRED BRAINS

THE ARTS

- Composer Elliott Carter celebrated his 100th birthday with a Carnegie Hall concert that included dozens of musical works he had written over the previous decade.

- Grandma Moses, one of America's most celebrated folk artists, generated over 3500 artworks between her 70s, when she began painting, and her death at 101.

- Martha Graham, the pioneer of modern dance, choreographed her last complete ballet, *Maple Leaf Rag*, at 96. She personally performed on stage at 76.

- Renowned architect Frank Lloyd Wright finished his design of the Guggenheim Museum in New York at 91.

- Master cellist Pablo Casals was asked, at 91, why he continued to practice. "Because I am making progress," he replied.

- Legendary choreographer Merce Cunningham debuted his most recent work, *"Nearly Ninety,"* at the Brooklyn Academy of Music at 91.

- Michelangelo was still at work on St. Peter's Basilica in the Vatican at 88. He was appointed architect of St. Peter's, the cathedral of the popes, at 72.

- Sculptor Louise Bourgeois created "*Spider*," which sold at auction for more than $4 million when she was 87. At the time, this was the highest price ever paid for the work of a living sculptor.

SCIENCE & MEDICINE

- Nobel Laureate Dr. Rita Levi-Montalcini founded her neuroscience research institute in Rome at 95 and oversaw its work until her death at 100.

- Dr. Marguerite Voit, whose research helped to document why some viruses can lead to cancer, continued her unprecedented work on cell biology at the Salk Institute at 93.

- Dr. George W. Comstock, perhaps the world's foremost expert on tuberculosis, oversaw community-based research on cancer and heart disease at the Johns Hopkins Center for Public Health Research at 92.

- Pioneering nuclear chemist Dr. Gerhart Friedlander of the Manhattan Project returned to Brookhaven National Laboratories to work on the famous GALLEX experiment in his early 80s.

- Albert Schweitzer continued working at his hospital at Lambaréné at age 90, after receiving the Nobel Peace Prize at 77 for his missionary work in Africa.

- Dr. Michael DeBakey, inventor of the artificial heart, ceased performing heart surgery at 90 to concentrate on laboratory research and cardiac postoperative care, which he continued to work on until his death at 98.

- Agricultural scientist Norman Borlaug, whose earlier work in food production saved hundreds of millions of lives, tackled a new variety of rust that threatened the world's wheat supplies at 90.

- Biologist Benjamin Duggar discovered *Aureomycin*, the antibiotic "wonder drug" that killed previously resistant bacterial infections, at 76.

LAW, LITERATURE & JOURNALISM

- Sophocles wrote *Oedipus at Colonus* at age 90. He penned his masterpiece, *Oedipus Rex*, on which Freud based his pioneering psychoanalytic theory, at 71.

- U.S. Supreme Court Justice Ruth Bader Ginsberg continued her work on the court until her death at 87.

- Oliver Wendell Holmes, Jr., known as the "Great Dissenter," was still writing landmark law on the Supreme Court at 90. He was first appointed to the court at age 61.

- Johann Wolfgang von Goethe finished the second part of his epic play, *Faust*, one of the most important works in German literature, at 83.

- At 82, Kurt Vonnegut, the novelist, playwright, poet and essayist, published *A Man Without A Country*, another of his many bestsellers.

- Satirist Art Buchwald continued to publish his syndicated newspaper column at 81. He once wrote that he favored pastries over exercise, which he considered dangerous to his health.

- Daniel Schorr, the last of Edward R. Murrow's CBS news team, continued his broadcasting commentary and analysis on National Public Radio into his mid-90s. He told USA Today: "I never expected to be working now, but I'll take it."

- William Carlos Williams, the pediatrician and poet, published *Pictures from Brueghel*, which was awarded the Pulitzer Prize when he was 79.

- Katharine Graham, the publisher, wrote her first book, *Personal History*, which won a Pulitzer Prize when she was 79.

- George Bernard Shaw was awarded the Nobel Prize in Literature in 1925 for *Back to Methuselah* at 69. He was at work on a comedy when he died at 95.

- Carl Sandburg was awarded the Pulitzer Prize for publication of *The Complete Poems of Carl Sandburg* at 72. He continued to write into his late 80s.

- Benjamin Franklin invented the first bifocal eyeglasses to help correct his own vision at 78. He was 70 when he helped draft the *Declaration of Independence*.

- Bertrand Russell, mathematician and philosopher, was awarded the Nobel Prize for literature at 78. He wrote his autobiography between the ages of 95 and 97.

- TV correspondent Mike Wallace and commentator Andy Rooney continued broadcasting on *60 Minutes*, the top-rated weekly news program, in their late 80s. Lesley Stahl was still on the air at *60 Minutes* at 81.

- Noah Webster published his famous *New International Dictionary* in 1828 at age 70.

BUSINESS, GOVERNMENT, ENTERTAINMENT & SPORTS

- Winston Churchill became Prime Minister of England for the second time at 77. He won the Nobel Prize for literature at 79.

- Nelson Mandela, four years after being released from nearly three decades in prison, was elected president of South Africa at 75, a post he held until age 80.

- Peter F. Drucker, the father of modern management, continued lecturing and consulting and published his 35th major book, *Management Challenges for the 21st Century*, at 95.

- Susan B. Anthony, the social reformer, founded the International Women's Suffrage Alliance in Berlin at 84.

- Mahatma Gandhi completed negotiations for Britain to grant independence to India at 77.

- Albert Schweitzer won the Nobel Peace Prize for his missionary work in Africa, also at 77.

- Golda Meir was elected Prime Minister of Israel at age 70 and held the post until age 74.

- George C. Marshall was awarded the Nobel Peace Prize for the famous Marshall Plan at 73.

- At 72, Israeli Prime Minister Yitzhak Rabin, 72, Israeli Foreign Minister Shimon Peres, 71, and PLO Chairman Yasser Arafat, 65, won the Nobel Peace Prize for their courage in carrying out backdoor peace negotiations in the Middle East.

- Thomas Edison headed the Naval Consulting Board in his mid-70s, directing research on antisubmarine warfare and technology. At 65, he produced the first talking motion pictures.

- Phineas Taylor (P.T.) Barnum co-founded the famous *Ringling Bros. and Barnum & Bailey* circus with archrival James Anthony Bailey at age 71.

- Ronald Reagan was first elected U.S. President at 69, Joe Biden at 77, and Donald Trump at 70. Nancy Pelosi left office as Speaker of the House at age 82.

- Sumner Redstone remained at the helm as Chairman of Viacom/CBS until age 93, four years before his death.

- Warren Buffett was still the Chairman & CEO of Berkshire Hathaway at 92. Rupert Murdoch was still running News Corp at the same age.

- Mother Teresa won the Nobel Peace Prize at age 69 and continued serving the needy until her death at age 87.

- Don Henley, Joe Walsh and Timothy B. Schmit, all 75, were still performing as the rock group, the Eagles, before huge audiences in the U.S. and overseas.

- Harrison Ford, age 80, played Indiana Jones for the fifth time in *Dial of Destiny*. Composer John Williams wrote the soundtrack at 91.

- Tony Bennett won a Grammy at age 95.

- At 82, Erlinda Biondic became the oldest woman to complete a 100-mile race.

- Lester Wright, at 100, set a new 100-meter dash record (26.34 seconds) for centenarians.

PART TWO

THE REINVENTORS

CHAPTER SEVEN

Navigating the Unretired Economy

As we saw throughout the first part of this book, some people work as insiders in unretirement, as employees within companies or organizations, while others work as outsiders, launching their own freelance ventures or entrepreneurships.

Some unretirees continue to do the same kind of work they've done since they graduated from college, while others—and we'll meet many in this part of the book—choose to reinvent the nature or structure of their careers.

Between them, journalists Kerry Hannon and Mark Miller have written many hundreds of articles and advice columns published in premier news outlets, such as the *New York Times, Reuters, USA Today* and

MarketWatch, concerning work and financial matters of importance to people in midlife and beyond. In fact, over the past several decades, they have earned well-deserved reputations as several of America's leading experts on these topics.

When they first began digging into them, the vast majority of Americans were planning to retire at some point in their lives or had already done so.

The track laid down by their predecessors remained essentially in place: you were born, went to school, worked or raised a family, then you retired full stop, few questions asked.

Fast forward to today, and everything's different or in the process of dramatic change, as the huge baby boom generation occupies what was once the retirement landscape.

By the year 2030, in fact, every member of this giant population will have passed the age of 65, with tens of millions in their 70s or early 80s.

For boomers, the prospect of working later in life is no longer "what somebody else does." It's a subject very much on their minds—for one thing, many can't easily afford a traditional retirement, and for another, as we've seen in previous chapters, many who can afford such a lifestyle, as one put it, would rather "be nibbled to death by ducks."

As these megatrends have developed, journalists Kerry Hannon and Mark Miller have studied and written about them.

Now that they're in their 60s, I wondered: how did they view the growing unretirement economy? How were they personally navigating it? What insights or recommendations might they have to offer the rest of us?

KERRY HANNON
NEWLY RELEVANT AND ENERGIZED

After reporting on age bias in the workforce for decades, perhaps no one was more surprised than Kerry Hannon when out of the blue, at age 61, she was recruited for a job as senior financial columnist at Yahoo.com, the news and information web portal.

At first, Kerry hesitated, concerned about abandoning the one-woman media company she'd built over the previous two decades—a structure through which she'd become nationally respected as a columnist, public speaker and author of more than two dozen books on careers for people aged 50 and older.

When Yahoo responded that she could continue doing all of this while also working for them, Kerry could hardly believe her ears.

> *They offered me a job with a salary that was probably more than I had ever made in my life as an in-house employee, plus the job was largely remote and came with benefits and paid vacation, which, as a self-employed woman, I'd forgotten even existed.*
>
> *And I've loved every day of the job since then. I love the people I work with. I feel valued, I feel relevant. My boss is two decades younger than I am, and it's just revitalized my work in a way that I never expected to happen in my 60s.*

While Kerry's experience of being suddenly scooped up by a leading-edge internet company may be unusual, the trend of which she is a part of has become unmistakable and widespread.

Where employers commonly "offload" older higher-paid workers, especially during economic downturns, the 2020-2022 coronavirus crisis shocked many companies and organizations into a stark, if belated, demographic reckoning: America's population was aging.

Peering out into the labor pool, employers were beginning to see the tip of a fast-approaching iceberg—the supply of educated, skilled younger workers was in decline due to a "fertility collapse" in the 1960s, while the population of experienced older people was surging, with some 3000 college-educated Americans entering their 60s each day.

In May of 2023, based on an in-depth survey of companies, large and small, the non-profit Transamerica Institute reported that the impact of these numbers was sinking in, leading an unprecedented 60% of employers to give "a great deal of consideration" to older job applicants during their recruiting efforts the previous year.

Kerry Hannon, who reported on this development on Yahoo.com, told me that she saw it as a window into what is yet to come.

Without question, I think we've had a huge transitional moment in the workplace and it's still evolving. You would not have seen this kind of opportunity 10 or 20 years ago. On both sides of the equation—employers and older workers—we're seeing this shift and it's fundamental. It's not going to go back because of the sheer demographics.

Because of the tight labor market, employers need people who have experience. They need to

*retain and attract them. Experienced people can hit
the ground running, they don't need to be retained
and they don't need to be upskilled. Any company
that's not focusing on this is going to be a loser—it's
the truth globally, not just in the U.S.*

Among the areas in which Kerry has long specialized
and been considered a national expert are the ways in
which older, experienced workers can go about seeking
or changing jobs.

What, I inquired, were her key recommendations
for older jobseekers, given the fresh opportunities in
the workplace?

She framed her advice this way:

TIP #1
RESEARCH & NETWORK

*You need the inside track because you're not going to get a
job from a job posting. So find out who the leaders are in
your field or community and see if you can get an infor-
mational interview and pick their brain for 20 minutes.
How did they get where they are? Where are the opportunities, where do they see growth, what's happening, who
else should I talk to? You can give the same advice to a
younger person, but one advantage for older jobseekers is
that we know more people. So don't be embarrassed to say:*

"Hey, I'm at this point, I'm looking for something to challenge myself, something to add value, to give back, whatever it is."

TIP #2
SEARCH YOUR SOUL

Ask yourself what you want to do and who you want to work for, not just who's going to hire you. Think about what companies and nonprofits you're interested in. Do you like their mission, do you want to be part of it? Think about your first job and the things you loved to do as a younger person. There's a thread through those memories that will link you to the kind of work you may want to do today. And remember that as an older person you should have the attitude that you have value to add. You're not retiring from something—you're looking for your next act.

TIP #3
BE FINANCIALLY FIT & CONFIDENT

If you have a lot of debt and you need to make money, that changes the whole scenario about the kind of work and salary you can accept. But when you're financially fit, it gives you confidence that opens your brain to opportunities, which makes you lean and mean, helps you to come

*off positively in interviews and gives you a vibrancy and
an edge.*

On the bottom line, Kerry advised: "be chill and keep
in mind that something could come out of left field, like
what happened to me—so be flexible and willing to try new
things. You're not 25 years old anymore or defined by this
moment in your life, so if things don't work out, so what?"

And what about retirement for Kerry Hannon?
When would it be in the cards? Never, she said, even if
her current Yahoo job turned out to be short-lived. "I
will always plan to work for pay in some fashion, writing
columns, books or speaking, as long as my health permits.
I love what I do, so it's not work at all, and it keeps me
curious and mentally engaged, and always learning
new things."

MARK MILLER
COMMITTED TO ENTREPRENEURSHIP

Although he had written expertly about subjects similar
to those that Kerry Hannon has focused on, including for
some of the same publications, when I spoke with journalist Mark Miller, he hadn't punched a clock as anyone's
employee for more than 15 years.

Mark took great satisfaction in having become entrepreneurial, which is the way he forever wanted things to be.

The creative control, the happiness quotient that comes with being able to chart your own course, being able to do exactly the work I want to do and not any of the work I don't want to do, that's fantastic. You have the pleasure of knowing that the wins are your wins, and the losses are your losses.

In the last corporate job he held before going solo, Mark persuaded his employer, the Chicago-based Tribune Company, to launch a new magazine and website focused on personal finance, careers, health and lifestyles for people over 50.

It really energized me that here was this big and growing audience of people who needed information and weren't being very well served by what the media was dishing out. It was one of those times where I felt like I was having an impact, and my work was meaningful to me.

The publication Mark helped start as an employee lasted only a few years, but when he walked away it was with a concept that he firmly believed had a bright future,

and one he thereafter honed into a journalistic business
he could call his own.

> *It feels like very mission-driven work to me to try
> to help folks at risk of decline in their standard of
> living later in life. I'm very passionate about the
> ins and outs of Social Security and Medicare and
> helping people understand how to get the most out
> of both. I love doing this kind of journalism, it's a
> great privilege.*

One of the approaches to shoring up late-life finances
that Mark has written about is the tack he's personally
taken—entrepreneurship—yet he cautions his readers to
be aware of the uncertainties this may bring. In his role as
a contributing columnist in the *New York Times*, Mark
has pointed out that "experts caution that transition from
full-time work to entrepreneurship not only takes longer
than you might expect, but also comes with twists and turns."

When we spoke further about this, Mark told me: "I
don't think self-employment is the answer for everybody,
not even for the majority."

But for those eager to pursue it, he provided some
thoughtful and pragmatic advice.

> *First and foremost, work from what you know and
> take advantage of your inherent resources—who you*

know and what you know, that's a great place to start. In so many cases, those who succeed as entrepreneurs are those who are continuing to play in the same space they've been in, they're just doing it from a different perch, and on a different income basis than before.

Next, do some serious research and adjust your expectations before rushing into the entrepreneurial fray.

Identify an idea and market in which your experience is viable. Get out and talk to people and test your idea and approach things with some flexibility and humility, because as you get going you may need to make adjustments. That's how it happened for me. I had two or three misfires, but one thing led to another, and while I was doing this, I met someone who introduced me to something that worked better.

Finally, be patient and willing to ride the roller coaster. That's a mindset shift from earning a paycheck as an employee. You need to adopt a whole new approach, both in terms of income and expenses. And if there's a way to have a buffer in there, whether it's a working spouse or a year's worth of liquid savings, that can be helpful.

And if you're in your late 60s or 70s, I would caution people not to finance their startup out of their retirement accounts, because you're rolling the dice on an important resource that you may need down the road.

Despite the caveats and risks, looking back from age 68, Mark said he had no regrets about the decision he made in his early 50s to take the entrepreneurial plunge: "Not at all, none," he said, "considering what's gone on in my industry, in the way that media has become destabilized and financially challenged."

Over recent decades, according to the Ewing Marion Kauffman Foundation, which studies business startup trends, many other mature professionals have come to feel the same way.

In fact, despite the youthful stereotypes, the composition of entrepreneurs in the U.S has been steadily aging, with the share of new entrepreneurs over age 55 rising to match the percentage of 20-to-40-year-olds who give business ownership a try.

And, as we'll see in the examples ahead, becoming your own boss, while simultaneously reinventing your line of work, can be a highly effective path to a successful unretirement.

CHAPTER EIGHT

Sparks of Reinvention

I first met Mona Stallworth in a program called "*The Joy of Reinvention*" that Kerry Hannon, Mark Miller and I led as a team at the Second Half Institute, a division of the executive education organization I founded several decades ago.

The Institute provides seminars and workshops for high-potential executives and professionals who have reached transition points in their lives and careers.

This described Mona to a tee—in her case, and that of many others in the room, the question at hand was whether to become full-stop retirees or join the growing number of unretired people of their age and level of accomplishment.

A business prodigy of sorts, in her early 20s Mona managed to secure a job at First Interstate Bank in Los

Angeles where, with only an associate degree, she quickly rose to a supervisory position in the international banking division.

"I have an analytical mind and I'm also very exacting," she explained, "and people recognized that in me, so I was promoted."

In her 30s, as computer technology first became essential in the workplace, Mona took the coursework required to work as a software programmer at Arco Oil and later as a systems analyst at Denny's, Inc., Burlington Air Express and a major aerospace company.

In her early 40s, she went back to school to earn a bachelor's degree and then rolled the dice as an entrepreneur. "I'd always loved business and inventing things," she said, "so that was just a natural move."

At one point in her 50s, she owned and operated two successful multi-level marketing firms, one selling baby products and another in the hospitality industry.

But while Mona's career soared, her personal life proved to be complicated—she was married and divorced twice while raising two children, a son and daughter, pretty much on her own.

Then, in her early 60s, she hit an iceberg: her third husband died unexpectedly and, several months after his passing, she was diagnosed and treated for breast cancer.

Her recovery was long and taxing—a "dormant period," she called it, in which she suffered through hours of exhaustion and days of panic attacks.

Eventually, however, the fog of lethargy began to lift.

That whole period, it was just not a good time for me—but out of that I decided I wasn't going out like this. It was after the death, after the cancer, that I started picking myself back up and remembering what I was able to do in my 20s, 30s and 40s. So there was a complete change in me and my perspective.

It was at this personal crossroads that Mona received an email from the University of California announcing that one of our Second Half Institute programs had been scheduled on a campus near her home.

She enrolled and joined us there in February of 2017, just short of her 67th birthday.

A STRUCTURE FOR THE FUTURE

In our program, we introduced Mona and her fellow participants to the building blocks of successful unretirement that we examined in Chapter Three.

With this formula on the whiteboard, we asked the group to begin considering the following questions:

What currently fascinates me or has always fascinated me and naturally drawn my attention forward?

What are ways in which I might turn my fascination into new forms of work that will generate flow experiences?

How can I structure an unretirement that not only benefits me personally but is also a gift to others?

The building blocks we provided, and the process of tackling these questions, sparked Mona's imagination, leading to a breakthrough that would soon redirect the course of her life.

That process just re-fired me. I walked away with such confidence and such determination, and it was like: "Yes, I can do this, this is doable." And what that meant was I knew that there were things inside of me that I needed to do, should do, and wanted to do. And facing death like I had made me realize I couldn't put this off any longer.

What Mona realized was that, in each career or business she had pursued in the past, she'd always been considered one of those uncommon individuals with the natural born skills to help others succeed—and that this was a gift that fascinated her and could become the platform for a rewarding future.

The decision she made during our program was to reinvent herself, put her fascination into action, and formulate a new business plan on which to structure her unretirement.

You know how it is with a natural gift—you just do it, and you don't think anything of it because it's natural for you to do. I did not understand the value and rarity of people who do what I do naturally until I heard about coaching and people getting paid to do what I'd been doing all my life.

Initially, Mona's concern was that the usual job title for people who did the type of work she had in mind was "life coach."

This was a term that did not sit well with her, as it had come to be associated with often inexperienced and

sometimes unethical practitioners who did little more
than hang out shingles and call themselves professionals.

*The problem I have is that there are coaches who
have not had any training other than a certificate.
They have no life experience, like I do. To be coaches,
they should be experts in something. However, most
of them have never been in business or started their
own business, so they can't give you anything more
than what you might read in a book.*

*And that's the problem with the life coaching
industry. If someone is really being challenged in
their lives or careers, if something's affecting them
financially, emotionally, psychologically, they need
someone that has been there and done that.*

*The wisdom that I've gained through actual
experience, through trial and error, by being on this
earth as long as I have—that's what I can bring to
a client.*

With this in front of mind, Mona put her consid-
erations aside, earned the necessary coaching industry
credentials, and leveraged her marketing skills to position
herself as the experienced professional she indeed was—a
former banker, systems analyst, entrepreneur and
successful parent.

Building her new venture took time and effort, of course, but she'd "been there and done that" before, as she pointed out, and eventually things took off.

Now I have clients on the east coast, I have some down south, and I'm working on having clients outside the country.

They're working people, they range from their 20s to about 59. Sometimes they need career advice, relationship advice, parenting advice. They are so talented in so many things, but they don't know how to prioritize in the way that I do.

I begin by asking them: "What's your end goal? Is it to make more money, to achieve more, what's your objective?" I don't give advice. What I do is ask: "Have you considered this, or have you thought about this?" And that way I'm telling them what I think, without actually giving them advice.

And how did she feel now, I inquired, when we spoke soon after her 72nd birthday—did she perhaps tire more easily than she had when she was younger?

To the contrary, I'm probably more energetic because I'm freer to be more creative, to use my energy more selectively, and therefore my energy level is higher. I think at this point in time, with the wisdom and understanding that came from taking the time to reflect on my past, I'm better now.

True, I don't move as fast, but then I realize that I don't need to. I'm not trying to be a swimmer or track star. I don't need to move fast. So putting everything in perspective, energy levels and all that, I'm better now than ever.

And what about the money she was generating at her rate of $100-150 per hour? Had it made a difference in her creature comforts or lifestyle?

I think the better question is: "Why did I decide that I really need to go back into the marketplace to make money?"

I live a modest life, my bills are paid, I have money to do things. But what I realized when I was struggling was that there were so many people in need, so many charities that I wanted to support. So that's when I recognized that I had a gift, an ability I wanted to use, and in doing that I was going to help my clients and, at the same time, make money to help others.

As I was getting older and I kept hearing people say "at your age" you shouldn't do this or that, it became clearer to me that I would never fully stop working because I refuse to believe or buy into that mindset.

I'm a work in progress, I still have a purpose, I still have a mission, I still have goals. And that gives you something to look forward to when a lot of people my age are just looking backward.

By reinventing herself and building a new enterprise with a highly generative edge, Mona had found a unique way to design what's commonly called a social entrepreneurship—one that benefits its founder while at the same time "paying it forward" to others.

This woman who once thought she was "all washed up" instead invented a powerful launch pad for a fulfilling unretirement.

CHAPTER NINE

The World's Oldest Business School

When Ken Mandelbaum stepped down as CEO of the New Jersey-based clothing company, Big M, Inc., he felt adrift and inept for the first time in his life.

> *I'm no longer running my company. I had 3000 employees and now I'm by myself. I didn't know how to do anything. I had to ask my wife to teach me how to use an ATM machine. What my assistant used to do in a day would take me a week, so I had to invent a whole new life.*

After the management consulting firm she founded fell apart, following the death of her Co-CEO, Jeanette Hobson needed a solution as well.

Let me give you my definition of the word retire. The root of the word is TIRE, and if I'm not tired, why would I need to retire? That's my feeling— when I get tired, then I will consider retiring.

Further west, in Colorado, Sam Reese thought he had retirement all figured out when he left the CEO position at the sales training firm, Miller Heiman.

The first three or four months were fun, then I knew that it wasn't going to work for me, but I kept faking it. It was just completely unfulfilling, and I think it was the action that was missing for me. I need to feel like I'm doing something important every day that has high stakes to it.

Three former CEOs, three different scenarios, one common solution—reinvent themselves and go back to work, this time on the faculty of the world's oldest business school.

Not old in the sense that it has ancient ivy-covered walls or that it's been around for a while, which it has, but because the average age of its faculty is 67 years old, with some individuals in their 90s.

Kevin Trout, former CEO of Grandview Medical Resources in Pittsburgh, characterized his colleagues this way: "People like us don't retire well—we made our money, we could sail off into the sunset, but we don't want to rest on our laurels, we want to stay engaged."

With a faculty of 1200, mostly older former CEOs, and a student body of 45,000, mostly current CEOs, the official name of this unusual institution is Vistage Worldwide, Inc.

Once inside, it's unlike any other business school you've ever seen.

FORGED IN FAILURE

Sam Reese, after flunking retirement in his 50s, went on to become Vistage's dean, or corporately speaking, its chief executive.

In his office, Sam keeps the memoirs of Milwaukee businessman Bob Nourse who, more than a half-century ago, out of frustration and desperation, brought together a group of local executives to tap into their advice as a group.

He was a failed consultant, he failed at the family business and he tried all sorts of things and had all sorts of anxiety trying to figure out how to be successful. So he brings these guys together, and says: "You guys all seem to be dealing with a lot of the same issues. What if we all come together and share ideas in a confidential setting?"

And it was only after about four or five meetings that people said: "Hey, should we pay you? This is really good, you're really helping us out."

What Nourse stumbled on, by happenstance, was a methodology called "issue processing," that became the foundation of Vistage's educational curriculum and remains its secret sauce today.

Simply defined: by bringing together non-competing executives in a confidential setting and encouraging them to let down, or better, pull out their hair while tackling each other's problems, unanticipated insights and solutions may emerge.

Explained Sam:

What a lot of younger CEOs today are really trying to figure out is what the future looks like. Am I gonna run this business or am I gonna sell it? And what happens is, we help them get towards clarity around where they really want to take their business.

What does all this have to do with older, former CEOs, who are no longer running the show and need something to do because they're not the retiring type?

They're the only ones with the time, patience and qualities, born of their own successes and failures, Sam told me, to make Vistage's programs work.

They definitely have this passion to help people, but it's not about their ego or résumé. They need to be past wanting to be in the spotlight. That's who these people are. They're not there to give you the answers—their role is to make sure to ask you the right questions so you can figure out what makes the most sense for you.

Nobody wants to join a group led by somebody who thinks they're a superstar with their own prescription for success—they want people who can share experiences, not tell you what to do.

And this, above all, is what distinguishes Vistage from just another business school.

WHERE BUSINESS SCHOOLS FAIL

In 2005, the year Hurricane Katrina, the costliest in history, slammed into America's gulf coast, another storm took aim at the vulnerabilities of the country's business schools.

Warren Bennis, widely revered as the "father of leadership education," launched a frontal attack in the *Harvard Business Review*, accusing business schools and their professors of ripping students off in previously untold ways.

At the top of the list, Bennis wrote: "Today it is possible to find tenured professors of management who have never set foot inside a real business, except as customers."

At a time when leadership and management skills were becoming increasingly crucial to the country's economic survival, and MBA candidates were paying many tens of thousands of dollars to attend top tier institutions, what they were getting in return, Bennis charged, was far more academic than reality based.

He wrote: "Business schools measure themselves almost solely by the rigor of their scientific research, but because so little of it is grounded in actual business practices, the focus of graduate business education has become increasingly circumscribed, and less and less relevant to practitioners. In fact, business is a profession, akin to medicine and the law, and business schools are professional schools—or should be."

Because Bennis, a leadership professor at USC for more than a quarter century, as well as a White House adviser, had the kind of real-world management experience he was writing about, his message hit home.

At the outbreak of World War II, he had been one of the youngest U.S. Army infantry officers to serve in Europe and was awarded both a Purple Heart and Bronze Star for valor.

In the 1960s and 70s, he served as Provost of the State University of New York and later as President of the University of Cincinnati.

"These were the most important learning years of my life," he told an interviewer. "In everything I did, my eyebrows were always raised. I learned a great deal about collaboration, modesty, and abdication of one's ego as a leader, about the idea that we, as an organization, are all in this together."

Nevertheless, for calling out American business schools the way he did, Bennis was labeled, by some, a sell-out and pariah.

"A few B-school faculty and deans attacked us as anti-science and nut cases," he blogged. In fact, "The dean of a top-five ranked school ripped my article to shreds, tossed the pages in the air and stomped noisily on them as if they were carrying a deadly virus."

But sadly, Bennis was right—business schools were widely failing the grade.

Worse, in 2014, two widely respected entrepreneurship experts, Jon Eckhart at the University of Wisconsin and James Wetherbe at Texas Tech, wrote a follow-up to Bennis' piece in the *Harvard Business Review* stating: "Ten years after (the Bennis) article was published, we believe this problem is even more acute."

They continued: "Business professors spend most of their time searching for research topics they think will interest other business professors. But, far too often, the research doesn't address the real problems of entrepreneurs, managers, investors, marketers and business leaders."

Which takes us back to Vistage Worldwide, Inc., where the educational business model is, well, strictly business.

MULTILEVEL PRESSURE COOKER

In the world of Vistage, nothing is theoretical—everyone is continually on the line to produce measurable results.

Sam Reese and his management team, based in San Diego, are under pressure to drive the growth of their company by increasing the size of its faculty and the number of students who pay to participate in Vistage programs.

Vistage's faculty, who are called "Chairs," are independent contractors whose earnings depend on recruiting and retaining students while facilitating group and individual coaching sessions.

Vistage's students, who are called "members," are responsible for taking away from their sessions whatever ideas, strategies and business wisdom are generated to keep their companies running as smoothly and profitably as possible.

THE WORLD'S OLDEST BUSINESS SCHOOL   151

Everyone's bottom line, in other words, is tied to everyone else's—it's about as unacademic and hard-knock as you can get, and that's the way they like it.

NOT THE RETIRING TYPE

Kevin Trout, whom we met briefly earlier, was in his mid-50s when he sold the Pittsburgh-based medical equipment business he had built from the ground up.

> *I had 60 employees and three offices, including one in Pittsburgh, one in Altoona, Pennsylvania and another in Charleston, West Virginia. By the time I sold out, we were doing over 14 million in annual sales, and 90% of the hospitals in our geography were our customers.*
>
> *As its owner, I identified with my business and the people that came to work for me, who I needed to take care of. So we had to be successful, and I was committed, like a thousand percent committed, to being successful in what we were doing.*

The people to whom Kevin eventually sold his business wanted him to stay on for an additional five years after the sale, and he agreed to, thinking: "Hey, I get to retire when I'm 59 and do whatever I feel like."

But not long after entering this arrangement, he began to get antsy.

I started thinking: "What am I gonna do?" I was a little restless, I didn't feel relaxed. Now that I was thinking about retirement, what did that really mean for me? I knew a lot of people who had just retired cold turkey and found things to occupy their time—they went golfing and skiing.

I ski, I scuba dive, but none of those things were what I wanted to do five days a week. And I thought: "Hey everybody in my family lives to a hundred. What am I gonna do for the next 40 years?" And I really liked coaching and mentoring as part of my role with my employees. And I thought: "How do I continue to do that?"

I had been in a Vistage group for 16 years when Vistage came to me and said they needed more Chairs in my area, and that's how I ended up being one. And I'm telling you, as much as I had a wonderful ride as a business owner, I enjoy this even more.

After training to be a Chair, Kevin recruited enough members in his area to fill four Vistage groups, each with about a dozen participants.

"Having been a sales guy my entire career," he explained, "I didn't find it that hard to connect with prospects. Others will tell you that recruiting members is the hardest part of being a Vistage Chair, but I didn't find it that difficult."

Kevin was 67 when I spoke with him and was working full bore for three weeks a month—preparing for and meeting with each of his Vistage groups, then following up with individual coaching sessions.

It was a rigorous, often demanding schedule, but one that he relished.

My overall energy level at this age is maybe slightly less than when I was younger, but my level of engagement and enthusiasm is higher than it's ever been. I get up at 5:30 in the morning. When I was working it was hard for me to get up before seven because I was a workaholic. I would work all day, every day, because I had to survive and keep the business going.

Now I get up and I'm enthusiastic to start the day, and I'll do some prep for group meetings and one-on-ones. Then by 6 p.m. I'm pretty well spent and done for the night. When I was younger, I would just keep going into the night, but I can't do that anymore.

During our conversation, Kevin took me on an abbre-
viated journey into Vistage's peer advisory "issue management process," which he and all Vistage faculty members
are trained to facilitate before taking on the job.

*Remember, our membership is made up of very
smart people, current CEOs and business owners.
But we all have challenges like: "How do I manage
this? How do I take advantage of that? How do I
deal with an underperforming employee?" So we
usually have two or three issues brought to the group.
Everything we talk about is confidential, and we
deal with each issue in the form of "how do I do"
this or that.*

*And then I go around the room, and everyone
shares their opinions or their guidance or suggestions, and there's a couple of rules to this. First, we
don't tell anyone what to do. The second rule is that
we're not looking for agreement or consensus—this
is not a debate.*

*Then I ask the original member: "What did you
hear? And what do you think you're going to do?"
Most of the time they say: "You made me see things
differently, you broadened my perspective and, as a
result, I thought I was going to do X but now I'm
going to do Y." And I say: "Okay, great, by when*

are you going to do it? Because we're gonna hold you
accountable, and we want an update next month."

So that's the way we move everyone forward, even
with the most difficult decisions they're faced with.

How does having been CEOs themselves, I asked,
make Kevin and his Vistage faculty colleagues the best
people to lead this process? Why not just have professional facilitators or psychologists do it—wouldn't they
be easier and perhaps less expensive to hire?

Because I've been through the whole thing—from
starting a business, to scaling it up, to selling it
off. So I get to apply a lot of what I learned, and I
can help members figure out the right questions to
consider in order to handle whatever they're facing.

And in their jobs, they have some really complex
issues to deal with. I don't have all the right answers,
but I do know the right questions to get them to the
right answers for themselves. That's the benefit of expe-
rience—and maybe at this point in time, of my age.

WORK AS ART

Up the eastern seaboard, in Elizabeth, New Jersey, Kevin's
age and workload might have seemed like a drop in the

bucket to Jeanette Hobson who, at 78, had been on the Vistage faculty for nearly three decades.

"For me, between my Vistage activities and the 50 private clients I'm coaching a month, it's a full-time job," she explained. "I also generally spend six to eight hours on the weekend, one way or another. I like it that way."

A former senior executive at the Bank of New York and, subsequently, founder and Co-CEO of a management consulting firm, Jeanette's best moments, she told me, came in times of intense challenge.

> I'm in the flow when I have a whole set of one-on-one conversations where I'm really tracking what the person is feeling and saying, and I'm able to get them to think differently about a problem or a business relationship in a way that's going to be more productive.
>
> Sometimes I'll go through eight or nine hours of these intense conversations, and at the end of the day not even realize what time it is—I feel totally energized by it. I'm helping the other person achieve what they want, and to me that's my definition of success.

At her age, even she was amazed by her energy level, which she attributed to the pleasure she experienced in her work.

I'm very appreciative that I have good health and I can do it, that my brain is working, probably not as well as 50 years ago but it's working. Why am I not tired yet? That's the question that I had been asking myself for several years when people asked me why I'm doing this and when I was gonna stop. And I never had a good answer.

And then I came across a quote in a book that said: "only humans can create art." And what I do is my art. And the reason why I keep doing it and that I'm not tired of doing it, is because I'm producing my art. My husband is 84 and he can sit for hours and paint. I can sit for hours doing one-to-one business coaching. Same thing, it's my art.

As we finished our visit, I asked Jeanette for her thoughts about the future and the prospects for the unretired Vistage Chairs she knew who were older than she—would there come a time when enough was enough?

When I look at my peers who are older than I am, some of them actually have physical disabilities that are age-related. But they still keep going, and they keep going because their minds are very sharp and their wisdom is intact.

There are some who have physical issues and they're in wheelchairs, but they still get themselves to their meetings and the members don't care. That's the thing. What Vistage members appreciate is more about wisdom than about anything physical.

When I don't have that anymore, I've told my members: "I want you to tell me because then I should think about retiring."

What about Kevin Trout in Pittsburgh—how long would he keep working?

Well into my 70s for sure. I don't think I'm planning on quitting cold turkey, but maybe I'll slow down a little bit. Instead of working three weeks a month, maybe I'll work two, and by the time I get to 75, maybe only one. I like being engaged and I know that I'll have a long lifespan, so I want to enjoy it.

And what was in the offing for Sam Reese, Vistage's chief executive, who tried retirement once before?

I have no plans to ever retire, I mean I know that I won't. I feel embarrassed about saying that, sort of like it's an ego thing. But I think for me it's feeling like I need a sense of purpose every day.

So when the time comes that I'm not fast enough to do this job, you will be talking about me being a Chair. From this, I will become a Vistage Chair, and I'll do that for as long as I can.

Somehow, I was not surprised when he said that.

CHAPTER TEN

Meeting the Couple of Tomorrow

Candace Kahn, age 77, and her husband Larry, 76, live in a sprawling home on a golf course that sits beside their swimming pool, surrounded by palm trees and mountains in one of California's premier retirement destinations.

They don't play golf, are rarely in the pool and have little in common with most of their neighbors.

What they both do is work—full time.

Sitting down with the Kahns at their kitchen table, in dappled morning sunlight, I was curious how this came to be.

Here they were—both in their late 70s and, from the look of things, sufficiently wealthy to have retired years earlier.

What exactly, I asked, was the holdup?

Candace: It's not for us. I can't imagine Larry not doing what he's doing. What would you do?

Larry: I don't even think about it. I mean, when you use that term, to me it's like people waiting to die.

Candace: Who wants to do that? Not me. I want to be active, always. I want him to be active.

Larry: To me, self-expression is being alive, and once that stops, you might as well be dead.

Candace and Larry work and express themselves in very distinct ways—and for the nearly five decades they've been married, it has always been this way.

They work out of the same house and, like much younger career couples, cross paths mostly on evenings and weekends. "We try to figure out when we can spend time together," Larry explained.

Trained as a consumer law attorney, Larry often worked up to 14 hours a day, operating the nonprofit that he founded; his office was at the north end of the house, with a small administrative staff based in other locations.

Candace, after a long career in business, had recently become an accomplished professional glass artist; her workspace, supplies and kiln, which heated to 1500 degrees, were located in a carefully renovated garage.

As is the case for many people, life had been a journey filled with twists and turns, some of them geographical.

But it eventually led to this atypical arrangement in which two nearly octogenarians lived, worked and felt as if they were in their 20s or 30s, while their retired neighbors seemed to be residing in another place and time.

NO ORDINARY RIDE

Candace Kahn's work life, she told me, started like those of many other young women who grew up in the New York metropolitan area in the mid-1960s.

The choices were that you could be a nurse, teacher or an airline stewardess. I started, but didn't stay in college, because I knew I was going to get married. But I felt like I needed something to fall back on, so I went to Katherine Gibbs secretarial school in New York City.

Then I worked for Sylvania Electric as a secretary and public relations assistant, then for a doctor as an office manager, and then my first husband and I moved to a small town in Virginia, where I became a real estate agent and broker.

The real estate work gave Candace her first taste of business, which she immediately found enticing.

I was doing real estate in a building right across from a store. I knew they were selling it, and I decided that I'm the one who should buy it, so I did.

Starting at age 24, I had a country store for a couple of years, then sold the inventory. I had learned that I was capable, that I could do pretty much whatever I set my mind to do. I knew the finance part and all of that from my brokerage training, so none of that scared me.

It was here, also, that Candace purchased her first horse—a luxury that the family in which she grew up could never afford.

At first, she rode strictly for "R and R," as she put it, from the daily stresses of running her retail store.

But, over time, her entry into the equestrian world led to something much more.

After she divorced her first husband and married Larry, they moved together to southern Oregon, a location that, at the time, felt like a good fit.

There, Candace developed a love for, not simply an occasional afternoon on horseback, but the sport of endurance riding—"riding from one point to another in the fastest amount of time possible," she explained, "without damaging your horse."

And business-oriented as she was, Candace transformed this passion into a company she named Action Rider Tack, Inc., an internet-based riding equipment firm she launched for $200 in her kitchen that grew to a million dollars in annual sales.

> *I had this niche of selling quality products to endurance riders, instead of just whatever Tom, Dick and Harry sells in a tack store. So it was more of a specialty business. They were all products that would make the horse comfortable—it was all about comfort for the horse during fifty or a hundred-mile rides.*

Larry, meanwhile, was navigating his own career and, subsequently, a reinvention of a very different kind.

NEGOTIATING SOLUTIONS

After graduating from law school at the University of Michigan, Larry went to the nation's capital, where he first worked for the Federal Trade Commission, prosecuting companies that were engaged in false advertising schemes.

Then, he moved on to a small law firm specializing in divorces, malpractice claims against physicians and personal injury cases.

While there, he gained a reputation as the "settlement guy."

I wanted to help people through personal legal crises—I call it "people law" instead of corporate law. What I would do is save both sides money and time by settling cases. I would contact the other attorney and give them a proposal in terms of what was reasonable.

Then I started my own firm called Negotiated Solutions, which was designed to keep people out of court through negotiation. Nobody had ever heard of anything like this before.

After some 30 years in the field, Larry had what he called an "awakening" or "otherworldly vision."

Something came to me from within in the middle of the night in January 2004. Prior to then, I'd given it absolutely no thought. And it was powerful. It wasn't so much a leap as an evolution of my own consciousness.

What Larry would do, he soon determined, was create, in place of a law firm, a nonprofit agency where people who couldn't afford lawyers could go for help, free of charge.

This was the start of an organization called Help Now! Advocacy, which had been funded by grants, donations and contributions of time by outside lawyers, since its establishment in 2004.

> *Most of our clients are either physically or mentally disabled or have some kind of deficit. They lack the educational and financial resources to fend for themselves.*
>
> *So the common thread of our work for them is negotiation, and we've negotiated to prevent power shutoffs, evictions, foreclosures, all kinds of things. For instance, we got a call from the United Way that said they had a woman who needed to have teeth extracted in very short order. Within 24 hours, I found an oral surgeon who was willing to extract her teeth for very little compensation.*

CALIFORNIA HERE THEY COME

After hopscotching the country in their younger years, when they reached their late 60s, the Kahns decided it was time to "settle down."

There was just one unresolved issue—Larry's nonprofit work was portable, but Candace, having sold her horse equipment business, needed a viable way to reinvent herself for the long haul.

It wasn't long before she discovered one.

I don't draw, I don't paint, and I never thought I had an artistic bone in my body. But I started doing fused glass, and I set up a studio and just started dabbling slowly.

Fused glass is taking pieces of glass, fusing them together in a kiln and then cutting them up and putting them together with other things to create sculptural pieces, wall hangings or functional pieces like bowls, plates, platters.

I've always had an interest in color and textiles, but I never thought I could do anything with any of that. It was a surprise. Then I started winning awards, and now it's a whole new career and business for me.

As we sat together over coffee and the Kahns shared their stories, I could sense that they were getting antsy—both had places to go and things that required their attention.

So I promised to keep them for only a few more questions.

Mark Walton: I get that you both enjoy what you're doing, but still, it's work and you're certainly old enough to call it quits.

Candace: I don't think of myself as working because it's more like fun. And with work, it's like eight to five, going back and doing the same thing day after day.

Larry: Like drudgery.

Candace: I don't think of it as work. I think of it as rewarding and being active and using my brain and whatever skill set I have.

Mark: Do you realize how unique a couple you are?

Larry: Yes, in fact I just had a conversation with a former partner with a big Washington law firm, and I tried to recruit him to work with me in my nonprofit, and he said: "Oh, I don't want to use my brain that much." And this guy is the same age as me! We have a neighbor who plays pickleball and other days she plays golf. We like to play pickleball sometimes, but it feels like a huge gulf between us and where she is in life. I can't relate, that's what I'm saying.

Candace: Different people have different goals, so if that's what they choose, that's fine, but it's just not something that we would choose for ourselves.

Larry: Well, except it's not really a goal, it's just something like: "Okay, now I'm entitled to sit back."

Candace: And take cruises, that kind of thing.

Mark: If you were asked to advise people, perhaps age 65 or younger, how to pursue the rest of their lives, based on what you've experienced, what would be your advice or guidance?

Candace: My advice would be to discover what really interests you and find yourself that way. I mean find something that would touch your inner soul, and then find or create something worth working on that involves that. In other words, experiment with your life.

Larry: I think people who do less than that are just waiting to die.

Candace: There's this illusion out there that you retire and life becomes peaceful. No, not for us anyway. I don't know what that kind of peace would even look like.

Larry: For us, for the kind of people we are, being busy at something that really matters, that's what's peaceful.

Today, it's hard to imagine that a dual income couple was a rare exception as recently as the 1960s, when men were the sole breadwinners in 70% of U.S. households with children.

By the year 2002, this was the case in only seven percent of families, once women and their daughters flooded the workplace, forever changing the face of the economy and American life.

In the grand scheme of things, the intervening decades were but a speck of time.

So perhaps the day isn't far off when reinvented retirement communities will advertise dual offices in every unit, when clubhouses will be converted into conference centers, and golf carts will be reserved for meetings with clients and customers.

When the "Sun Cities" and the "Leisure Worlds" will become "We Work" villages filled with *un*retirees like Candace and Larry Kahn.

PART THREE

THE CREATIVES

CHAPTER ELEVEN

The Art of Unretirement

I first became intrigued by the possibilities of unretirement after getting to know[Sherwin B. Nuland.]

He was 77 years old on our first visit, and was nearing 82 on the next, which turned out to be our last in-person encounter.

Sadly, he died of cancer not long afterwards.

Shep, as he liked to be called, was different things to many people—a masterful surgeon, an award-winning author, a much-loved husband, father and grassroots philosopher.

For me, particularly as a writer, he personified the very essence of what an important unretirement can be.

EVERY LIFE STAGE IS DEVELOPMENTAL

My trips to see Shep somehow felt like coming home.

He lived in a suburb of New Haven, Connecticut, in a New England style house not unlike the one in which I'd grown up.

I was originally connected with him by a mutual friend, and he and his wife, Sarah, welcomed me as though I were part of their family.

Shep's study was upstairs on the second floor—a large and comfortable window-filled space, replete with heavily-stocked bookshelves on all sides.

It was in this room that he had written 10 books of his own, to that point, including one that a dozen years earlier had received the National Book Award, the highest literary honor in the United States.

But that wasn't what brought me here this time around—I was interested in his most recent book, *The Art of Aging: A Doctor's Prescription for Well-Being,* which had been published since our last visit.

I was approaching age 62 at the time and, frankly, frightened by the title.

I didn't think of myself as aging but was increasingly aware that I was getting older, and what I read in his pages struck me like a lightning bolt—I'd never heard anything like it before.

Clearly directing his words to people around my age and beyond, he had written:

> From here on, we must play only to our strengths. The later decades of life become the time for our capabilities to find an unscattered focus, and in this way increase the force of their concentrated worth.
>
> Living longer allows us to continue the process of our development. Unlike most other animals, the human species lives long beyond its reproductive years, and continues to develop during its entire time of existence.

Until the moment I first read this, I had never thought of my 60s and 70s as a *developmental* period.

Rather, I had always viewed these decades as the beginning of an inevitable downhill slide—this is what I had witnessed in the lives of my grandparents, my parents and other older people I'd been around, and assumed it universally so.

But, as we settled into our easy chairs, here was this remarkable 81-year-old telling me, from personal experience, that I had it all wrong.

> *I've never thought of 60 or 70 as the downhill slope—they're developmental stages. And ever since I've been in my middle years, perhaps in my late*

30s, I began to think of, well, I'll use that word, the wisdom of older people.

I began to think of the fact that the knowledge we have is essentially like a tree. Everything we know is hung on the branches of the tree, and as we age there are more branches and therefore more things you can hang.

Then, drawing from his nearly encyclopedic memory, Shep recited word-for-word several lines from a poem by Robert Browning, which I had heard before but to which I'd never paid much attention.

Grow old along with me!
The best is yet to be,
The last of life, for which
the first was made:
So, take and use thy work;
Amend what flaws may lurk.
Look not thou down but up!

What kind of *work* was it that I should "take and use," I wondered, as I absorbed these lines, and Shep sat quietly by.

I'd already had two careers—one as a broadcast news correspondent, the second as an executive educator, and

I felt both fortunate and gratified that both had played out as well as they had.

What was it that Robert Browning and Shep Nuland would have me do now? Find a new career? Launch another business? How, where and what about?

As if sensing my frustration, Shep repeated something he'd once written to me in a letter: "We may lose our bodily strength as we get older, but we don't lose our creativity until our eyes are closed by the minister or the doctor, even if it's at age 101."

Next, he recounted a story, which he had included in his book, about a public institution for the aging he'd been invited to visit in Paris.

There were 2000 people there, and they ranged from people who had been laborers to people who had been professors and all kinds of other high-level jobs. There was a wonderful psychologist who worked there, and he decided that the secret of an old age that provides happiness is creativity—so he developed a plan.

He recruited artists from all around Paris and asked them to volunteer at this institution for the aged. He got the administration to convert a number of the patient care units into studios, or ateliers, as the French call them. And anybody who wanted could study painting with an artist. I'm not talking about arts and crafts—I'm talking about really serious studies.

And he was stunned at the hundreds of people who had never painted before, who would use these ateliers. Everybody had a key of their own. If you woke up at three in the morning and couldn't sleep, you could work on your painting.

At the time I was there he'd been at it about 15 years. He had thousands upon thousands of paintings. Some of them were glorious, some of them were terrible, but it didn't make any difference. It was the sense of creativity, and I think creativity is so much the secret of what we're talking about here.

Each of us has to feel within himself, herself, that they're making something. It doesn't have to be a structure, it doesn't have to be a painting, but it's something that comes out of their distinct personality.

In a world overflowing with homespun theories and unsubstantiated opinions, Shep Nuland stood out—he knew exactly what he was talking about.

IT BEGAN WITH A PHONE CALL

In his early 60s, after nearly four decades in medicine, Shep had grown increasingly concerned about the sustainability of his skills in the operating room.

He had noticed over the years that other surgeons, starting at age 61 or 62, had begun to slow down, sometimes requiring an extra half hour or longer to perform routine procedures.

"Maybe it was psychological," he thought, "but I didn't want that to happen to me and felt like there was something going on in my head that was saying: "Hey buddy, pretty soon there's another adventure lying in store for you."

What this was, he didn't know—until the phone call.

I was seeing patients in the office and my secretary walked into the examining room, which she never did, and she said there's a man on the phone who says he is an agent, a literary agent.

And I spoke to this fellow on the phone, and he said: "You know, I've got an idea for a book, and we've been looking around for someone to write this book." And he said: "I went around to editors asking for names of people who could write the book, and your name came up. So here I am, and I want you to write this book."

Shep's name had come up because he had written an earlier book of physician biographies, as well as articles and medical studies that had been well received in professional circles.

But this was a whole different animal.

He said to me: "Do you know there's no book for medical students, or for the general public, on dying? Not the emotional aspects of dying, but the physical aspects. What happens to your body? What happens to your brain, what happens to your heart, your tissues?"

And he said they needed someone who was very well acquainted with the process of dying and death to write such a book, essentially the physiology of dying. And they were gonna call this book "How We Die."

So I decided to take a year off and, as I planned it, I would write a chapter on each of the major diseases, like cancer, stroke, heart disease, suicide and accidents, matters of this nature. That was all I knew. And I had no idea what I would write after that, except that a lot of it would be from my personal experience.

Sitting at his desk each day over the next year with pencil and pad—his preferred method of writing—Shep discovered two things about himself.

First, that he was a much more creative writer than he had ever previously believed; second, that he was fascinated by, and truly loved the daily writing process.

> *It gives me an extraordinary feeling that I can only call aesthetic. It was the same feeling I had when I operated. I loved the technical aspects of surgery. I loved the tissues in my hands, I loved to hold instruments in my hands, I loved to stitch and tie. That's the way I feel about writing.*
>
> *It's something that brings to me what psychologists have called the "flow sensation." You really detach from anything else. You have the sense that something is coming out of you. It is a physical sense, it's an emotional sense. The outside world is lost to you, and when you're through, and only when you're through, do you realize that you feel like you've been sitting in some Athenian glade talking to Socrates.*
>
> *Part of my sense of happiness when I write, part of my flow, of my sense of cadence and rhythm, is the feeling that I'm giving something to the world.*

Shep's book was an enormous success. *How We Die: Reflections on Life's Final Chapter* remained on the New York Times bestseller list for 34 weeks, was named a Pulitzer Prize finalist and won the National Book Award for nonfiction in 1994.

> *And the result is that I've written about nine more books since that time. My notion, which came to me over several years, is that each of us has somewhere deep down in the unconscious mind, memories, knowledge, creativity and even wisdom that we don't know we have.*
>
> *And if we sit down and try to put this into form, then, lo and behold, it comes up from this secret place, this source within us. And we each need to take that thing on, put that thing to work. It's your project really—it's the project for the rest of your life.*

DOCTOR'S ORDERS FOR UNRETIREMENT

In theory, I could appreciate Shep's point—in one form or another, we're all inherently creative. And if we can locate the "secret place," as he put it, the original source of our creativity, we can tap into and work with it.

But I had questions: Where do we look for this creative wellspring? How do we know when we've found it? How difficult will it be to transform this, as Shep put it, into "the project for the rest of our lives"?

Unsurprisingly, he was filled with answers.

Look To Your Childhood

We can't locate our creativity with a scalpel or a CT scan, Shep said—but when we were little, it was one of our best friends.

It was working through us when we were making up games in the playground, putting on shows in the living room, turning towels into capes, dressing up and pretending we were other people or comic book characters.

"Looking back, I was always fascinated with writing," he told me.

I can remember my first piece of nonfiction. I was eight years old and there was a carnival on a vacant lot. I'd never seen anything like this. I went by myself, and I saw these rides and pitching pennies and who knows what. And I just had to write about it.

So I took a pencil and wrote as fast as I could, my description of this. And one day seven or eight years ago I found it again. I've kept this in my library to remind me that this is what I began doing at the age of eight and I've done ever since.

For you, it will likely be something else. First, you need to discover, or rediscover, how you expressed your creativity or wanted to be creative as a kid. Were you interested in writing, painting, acting, music—what was your creative talent or fascination back then?

Look To Early and Middle Adulthood

Next, Shep advised, examine what may have happened when you began and were engaged in your career—[what did you put aside, or perhaps suppress, in order to be successful?]

> *I think our humanity often gets stunted in our occupational years. You come out of college, and you begin working for some big stock brokerage concern, for instance, and everything that has come before is laid aside.*
>
> *You become a stockbroker, or a lawyer, executive, doctor or whatever, and all your energies are devoted to that. And your vacations are in places where those kinds of people go.*
>
> *As you think back on this, you begin to rediscover who you were many years ago, with that wide range of interests that you gave up to become whatever you became.*
>
> *So now you should begin looking for those things and expand the horizons of possibility. As you're getting older, you can bring those horizons back into focus and see what might be most interesting, and most rewarding, and what you can actually do as opportunities appear.*

Start Soon and Buckle In

"Remember," Shep said, "that every stage of your life has been prepared for by everything that came before it." But each next step requires "overcoming inertia" and a commitment to move forward.

> *As I said earlier, it's your project, really, it's the project for the rest of your life. It's hard work. It's too easy to give in to inertia, and that's where those of us who've worked very hard all our lives have an advantage.*
>
> *A lot of people don't work very hard all their lives, and it's very easy for them to slip into this kind of steady state of nothing or decline. And go to that sunbelt place with their "Go to Hell" pants and play shuffleboard or whatever it is.*
>
> *But those of us who've had challenging things to do in which every year brought greater growth in our profession, are much more likely to be insistent on greater growth once we're older. We're not going to sit still for decline.*
>
> *Yes, it takes enormous motivation, but the need for motivation becomes less as the years go by, because once the initial inertia is overcome, this thing has a momentum of its own.*

As the afternoon sun dropped below the windowsills, I could tell that Shep had tired, ever so slightly, of sharing so much with me—after all, his 82nd birthday was not far off.

But the physician, writer and great communicator within him still had a few more thoughts to add about life and his prescription for well-being.

> *To begin with, life is not short despite what they tell you—in fact, life is long. Americans now live to an average of 75. That means that half of us are gonna live well beyond that. Some of us are gonna live well into our 90s.*
>
> *If life is actually one long passage, that passage has to be useful and happy for all of it, or in the end, it will have been in vain. So we should begin thinking early about what the latter part of that passage will be.*
>
> *Happiness can be defined in any number of ways. But primarily it is a sense that life is rewarding. It is rewarding in the work that we can do, it is rewarding in the attachments we have to other people as individuals and as members of society.*
>
> *To me, that's what happiness is.*

I had no idea, as I put my tape recorder and notes away, that this would be the last time I would see Shep

Nuland—he didn't mention his cancer prognosis and seemed to be in good spirits, as always.

What I did know was that I would never be the same for having known and spent time with him, and that I now understood what it genuinely meant to live happily ever after.

CHAPTER TWELVE

When Creativity Suddenly Appears

Crisscrossing the U.S. while doing research for this book, one of the places I found myself was deep inside a North Carolina pine forest where giant metal flowers appeared to be growing out of the ground.

Had these lovely figures been planted there or taken root on their own in the moist soil?

The stems were so lifelike, and the petals so vibrantly colored, that my experience of walking among them was simultaneously natural and surreal.

It's often said that powerful art evokes surprising emotions and sensations.

And in a way I couldn't grasp at the time, I felt comforted—it somehow seemed as though the metal flowers and their surroundings belonged together, that their intermingling made natural sense.

Several weeks later, 2500 miles west of that forest, I had an entirely different feeling.

Standing in the lobby of a Los Angeles office building, I sensed a bolt of energy surging through me as I gaped at large high-contrast photographs of Cuban dancers swirling through the streets in Havana; of American construction workers pirouetting on girders hundreds of feet in the air; of Parisian bicyclists kissing as they crossed the Seine.

Far more unexpected, even, than my experiences of these highly distinct creations—the calming metal flowers and the powerful photographs—was an astonishing fact.

These impactful works had been created by people who had never produced anything like them before or considered themselves capable of doing so.

At a point in their lives when they might well have retired, they discovered creative skills and abilities they never knew they had.

- **How did this happen?**
- **Is it possible that we all harbor within us hidden skills and abilities?**
- **Is a particular mindset or perspective required to uncover and put these capabilities to work?**

In this chapter, we'll see how Rita Spina, a burned-out clinical psychologist, unpredictably became a much-in-demand environmental artist, known for creating, among other works, the remarkable metal flowers I encountered.

And we'll visit with Gil Garcetti who, after being fired from one of America's highest profile legal positions, suddenly began to produce powerful photographs that would grace the walls of businesses, galleries and museums nationwide.

Through their stories, we'll see how previously undiscovered skills and abilities enabled them to reinvent themselves, rather than retiring, and we'll explore the neuroscientific reasons why almost any of us could be capable of such transformations.

RITA K. SPINA
REDISCOVERING LONG FORGOTTEN SKILLS

In her 60s, Rita Spina received an emergency phone call, informing her that her 25 years of marriage had come to a tragic end—her husband had died from a heart attack while playing tennis with friends.

His passing, Rita told me, left her totally on her own.

She said: "I went through a really tough time because he had set the foundation between the two of us, you know, the foundation that we were going to live on. After he was gone, there was no guideline for me because he wasn't coming home."

Rita's personal crisis coincided with a career breakdown that had been brewing for some time—after more than four decades as a clinical psychologist, she no longer enjoyed the work she once loved.

> *What I really needed was to turn away from it. I closed my old psychology books and stuck them in a big box in the attic, and that was the end of it.*
>
> *I still wanted to accomplish something, to continue developing myself. That's the way I'd always been. But I had no idea where I was going, no thoughts in my mind.*

Where Rita decided to go was to Oregon to visit with her daughter, who was living in Portland at the time.

On what was to have been a leisurely drive from the city to the Oregon Coast, she found herself surrounded by huge logging trucks on the highway, and was outraged by the payload they carried.

Years later, recalling the experience, her voice still trembled.

> *The loggers had cut down all the historic old growth forests, and in the most beautiful spaces there was nothing left but stubs. And I was just struck by it,*

and actually felt nauseous about it. Our heritage, as a country, was forever lost. And when I came back home to North Carolina where I lived, I just couldn't forget it.

Over time, her emotions evolved, and she began to experience a sense that there was something she needed to do about what she'd observed.

But what skills or opportunities did she, as a psychologist, have to express her feelings—and who would pay attention?

Back home, Rita developed a new habit of taking long and seemingly aimless walks through the southern pine forests behind her house.

And for reasons that were yet unclear, she began collecting natural debris, particularly fallen branches with interesting shapes, which she stored in her garage.

She wondered what was happening to her—why was she gathering this stuff?

Walking in the forest, I would collect old pieces of wood and stuff like that, and it felt somehow or another like it was all related, all focused on what I had seen and experienced in Oregon.

At about the same time, I also began going to junkyards and picking up discarded things that

*had been man-made, things that reflected change
and technological progress.*

*Back in my garage, I began to put these elements
together in three-dimensional pieces you might very
roughly call artwork. And I began to get ideas about
how wood and man-made material played off one
another. I found, for example, that if you turn
an old, discarded golf club upside down, you can
transform it into an iron flower.*

*And I thought: "Maybe I could create art that
demonstrated how the natural world and the
man-made world could peacefully coexist, without
anything being destroyed. And this became the
concept and message I somehow wanted to send if I
could figure out how.*

Rita had always been an art lover.

As a young girl, she'd pored over art books and
attended classes at the Parsons School of Design in New
York City, where she grew up.

But she'd never seriously considered art as a career
path. Instead, she put her creative passions aside to earn
a PhD in clinical psychology, which she practiced for
decades in school, corporate and private settings.

It took the shock of Oregon's clear-cutting experience
to reawaken the long-suppressed artist inside her.

*As a kid, what had been stored in my psyche was
that someday, when I had time, I would again start
to explore that piece of myself, which was the world
of art. And here I was finally doing that!*

As her imagination conjured up potential art forms,
artistic skills she had loved learning in high school, like
design and brush painting, seemed to come back quickly.
At the same time, she began learning new skills, such as
sculpting and welding, which sparked her interest.

Perhaps as importantly, she began to discover that the
community where she lived was filled with creators, some of
them accomplished artists who took her under their wings,
helped her to hone her abilities and eventually persuaded
her to display her work at a local art exhibition and sale.

That's where everything changed.

*It was a situation where the seven other people in the
exhibition had been artists for many years. Here I
was, a brand-new person. And somebody bought my
first piece—I was totally shocked.*

*Now all of a sudden, I felt like I was a genuine
artist. And it was at that point it became a new
career for me.*

Rita never returned to practicing psychology. Instead,
she set up a small studio in her home, which also served

as a gallery where visitors could view and purchase her creations.

Over the next several years, her work started to be featured in exhibitions, studio tours and competitive art shows throughout North Carolina, where she gained a reputation as an artist with a message—that nature and mankind *can* beautifully coexist—if only we make a conscious effort to bring them together.

WHAT EXPLAINS THIS?

As Rita indicated in our conversations, she was astounded that, after years of viewing herself solely as a psychologist, she had suddenly begun creating artwork that people wanted to own.

She said: "I didn't think anybody would want it, so it was amazing to me that somebody bought it, because I just figured that I would take it home with me after the show."

Perhaps her biggest shock was that she could not only envision her artwork before she made it, but was able find within herself, or learn to develop, the professional-level artistic skills necessary to craft what she'd imagined into material form.

Turns out, she shouldn't have been surprised.

Why? Because no matter how many times we've heard the bromide, "you can't teach an old dog new tricks," or been led to believe it, it's scientifically untrue.

Pioneering neuroscientist Michael Merzenich, whom we met in Chapter Six, was the first to provide solid evidence of this, when he revealed his discoveries about neuroplasticity—the brain's ability to continuously remodel and improve itself *if*—and here's the key—*if* we continue to teach it new tricks.

If, like budding artist Rita Spina, we make the effort to put latent, perhaps long-forgotten, skills to work, while continuing to learn and develop new ones, seemingly amazing things can occur.

When I met with Merzenich, this was one of the areas we delved into.

Mark Walton: One of the things I've seen in some of the people I've studied are leaps in abilities— that is, they seem to quickly develop hidden creative skills or abilities in areas you would never expect. Is it your belief that we may all have hidden skills and capabilities?

Dr. Merzenich: Of course we do, and we also always have within us the ability to step life up a notch in whatever we're doing, to carry ourselves to a higher level of operations or extend our operations.

As we've discussed, the brain is continuously changing and revising its wiring as a consequence of what we do. And each time you acquire a new skill or ability, or take on a new set of challenges that requires new learning on a substantial level, the brain is remodeling itself.

We know that we can acquire a new skill or ability right up to the last days of our life. We know that we can improve if we really work at something at any point in life, and that's another way of saying that this gift, this ability, is with us for the duration of our life.

Mark: *So you're saying that you've seen this kind of thing before, this kind of transformation in older people, and that there's a neuroscientific basis for it?*

Dr. Merzenich: *Absolutely—there are many instances of this in history, and we probably all know somebody who at some point in their life has basically taken things up to another level. And now they are suddenly doing things in a magnificent way that they could not imagine they could do. I believe that almost every one of us has latent abilities that we've never fully exploited and that later in life you can transform yourself.*

Mark: When you say later in life, can you put an age on it?

Dr. Merzenich: Well, I mean this could happen at any age. But it often happens in individuals who, at some period of their profession, or in the mainstream of life, determine to redefine themselves or finally exploit the thing that's been in the back of their mind—the thing they've always enjoyed doing or wanted to do. If it really matters to you, it really matters to your brain, and what seems like miraculous change can happen.

GIL GARCETTI
FINDING SKILLS HIDDEN IN PLAIN SIGHT

In my conversation with Merzenich, the other person I mentioned, besides psychologist Rita Spina, was a high-profile attorney who uncovered previously hidden skills as remarkable as hers, when he was suddenly struck by a career crisis of his own.

If the name Gil Garcetti rings a bell, it's likely because his son, Eric, was mayor of Los Angeles for two terms and, years before that, Gil was the Los Angeles District Attorney whose office prosecuted the notorious O.J. Simpson murder trial.

Several years after Simpson was acquitted, voters threw Gil out of his job.

He was 59 years old—the age at which he might still have gone to work at a big Los Angeles law firm for a few years, or he could have retired.

Neither option was appealing, Gil told me: "The day after my election loss, I'm emotionally bruised, angry and upset. I didn't only want to be able to contribute to my family, I also wanted to make a difference in the world, even if it was just a tiny, tiny bit."

While he didn't have a clear plan, he did have a hobby, maybe even a bit of an obsession, to hear him tell it.

> *I had started carrying a camera with me wherever I went right after my daughter was born. And I got in the habit of always having it with me, because you never know what you're going to see.*
>
> *I loved taking photographs. I found satisfaction and a personal reward in it. I wasn't doing it for any other reason. I'd never had any training, although I did start going to an adult night class in photography at one point. But I wasn't thinking that I was going to become a professional photographer at any time.*
>
> *It was just a hobby—an intense hobby.*

What Gil didn't fully recognize was how fine a photographer all this ad hoc practice had made him. Or how the skills that he'd developed as a prosecutor—his ability to rapidly assess and absorb details at any scene or location—had given him an advantage that other photographers might never have.

> *As a prosecutor, I was always seeing things that other people would look at but didn't see. And I'd say: "Well didn't you see that? You were looking right at it!"*
>
> *I'm not saying that I'm any better than them, but I saw something there that was of interest. It could be the design, the geometry of it, whatever was intriguing to me. I wanted to capture that for myself, but I also wanted to share it with others.*

Six months after leaving the D.A.'s office, everything seemed to come together for Gil in a moment of perfect synchronicity—he found himself, with his camera, in the right place at precisely the right time.

> *It was a happenstance encounter. I'm at a meeting downtown. A volunteer board that I'm on, and I'm leaving, starting to drive home.*
>
> *I'm between the Dorothy Chandler Pavilion and the Walt Disney Concert Hall, which was then*

under construction. And I look up and see this one ironworker who is literally on all fours, crawling over a high arch beam way, way up in the sky. And I thought: "Whoa, wait a minute, I have to photograph this guy!"

So I took a few snapshots and then came back the next morning with bigger camera equipment. And from across the street, I saw this guy again, way up in the air. To him, he was just doing his job. To me, he looked like a daredevil.

I realized: "This is marvelous! Look at the beauty of this geometry of the iron, the raw steel that's there." But I'm way across the street, how do I get on site? So I made a phone call and eventually made a connection with some of my union friends, and they let me onto the construction site.

Over a period of several months, Gil kept returning to the construction site and, at their request, started giving copies of the photos he was taking to the "daredevil" workers who were his subjects.

They were flattered and flabbergasted—to their eyes, Gil's photos were truly excellent. So much so, that they kept insisting that he compile and publish a book of his work.

They promised him that the structure they were constructing was destined to become a world-famous building, and that everyone was going to remember Frank Gehry, the architect who designed it, but nobody was going to remember them.

At first Gil resisted, afraid that anyone outside of the tight-knit construction team would see his photos for what they were: the work of an amateur, a neophyte, who didn't know what he was doing.

But the workers kept nudging him on.

I finally said: "Okay, I'll do it." My fear was that some publisher would take my notoriety as the former District Attorney and publish the photographs for a quick buck and then I'd get panned. And that would be the end of my photographic career, if I was ever going to have one.

But as it turned out, I was convinced by people at the Los Angeles Philharmonic, whose home would be the new Disney concert hall, as well as several respected critics, that the photographs would stand on their own. Forget me or who I was. So that's how my first book, titled "Iron: Erecting the Walt Disney Concert Hall," came out.

Not long after, I knew things in my life had really changed when two things happened almost immediately. One was that the Los Angeles Times, which was my nemesis when I was the D.A., suddenly couldn't say enough good things about me as a photographer. They were praising me to the hilt.

The other was that, out of the blue, a major law firm contacted me, because they had seen the book, telling me that they wanted to buy ten or twelve photographs.

And I thought: "Hey, they wouldn't offer the kind of money they did for these photographs unless they thought they were really worth it, because law firms are notoriously cheap." So that was a reaffirmation to me that maybe I really did have something here with my photography.

Three years, and numerous other photo projects, books and public exhibitions later, Gil earned the right to be totally confident of this, when the prestigious *American Photo Magazine* named him one of the country's four master photographers.

WHAT'S THE X-FACTOR HERE?

When all is said and done, is there a secret, some unique element that can drive dramatic, unexpected transformations like Gil and Rita's?

A distinctive factor that might allow any of us to tap into previously unrecognized skills and abilities?

For the answer, I turned again to Dr. Michael Merzenich, the neuroscientist who had literally mapped every inch and assessed every chemical running through the human brain.

Mark Walton: What's the most important thing, or what are the most important things that we need to do in order to make these great leaps in our abilities? How do we think or program ourselves, or train ourselves or exercise our minds?

Dr. Merzenich: You need to be working at something you care about—something you love. It has to matter to you. One of the ways to think about how you could define where you belong, or how you could strengthen or elaborate yourself is to ask: "Well, what's important to me? What's exciting to me? What's rewarding to me? What makes me happy?"

One of the really interesting things that we commonly see when people transform themselves is that they're not just doing something at a mundane level. We often see that they've found what they were really meant to do in life, and they take a great leap forward in the extension of their potential and possibility. They suddenly move into the domain that they were really constructed for.

Let's say you've always had a dream that you would really love to do something. If that's so, then it's worth pursuing, and that's the way to think about it. Because what that means is that when you get into the activity, if it is in fact continuously rewarding and positive, you will be changing your brain in ways that empower you.

Through decades of studying how the brain operates, Merzenich scientifically established and quantified what people like Rita Spina and Gil Garcetti learned from personal experience: that nearly all of us may have high-level creative skills and abilities we're not aware of—talents that we can develop, not simply to enjoy or play around with, but to seriously reinvent ourselves, instead of retiring.

CHAPTER THIRTEEN

The New Creative Marketplace

Gym Tan Miller, born and raised in Singapore, spent three decades as an executive in the international fashion business, including as fashion director of the Espirit brand and president of DKNY Jeans international, where she headed up all operations outside the United States.

In her late 50s, Gym moved to the San Francisco Bay Area, where her husband's family was located and her daughter was planning to attend college.

Her work life, which until then had developed beautifully, suddenly hit a brick wall.

"My career didn't really translate into Bay Area brands," she told a fashion editor, "because they had more of a domestic focus. So I started consulting and had to learn new things, like selling myself and using various technologies—it was tough to start a new life in my 50s."

When Gym reached her 60th birthday, still frustrated and unfulfilled, her daughter, May, a social media devotee, raised a possibility: Why didn't Gym share her daily outfits on TikTok and, by doing so, re-enter the fashion industry in a new and different way?

"Mom, why don't you just start posting an outfit a day?" she asked. "I love your style. My friends all love your style. Do it for fun and see where it goes."

After a few lessons in basic video production, Gym took on the challenge.

"I approached TikTok as a way of exercising my passion," she explained. "I used the experience I had in the fashion world in a personal way—assembling outfits, adding accessories, etc. I didn't know if it would go anywhere, but, within three weeks, I had 10,000 followers."

A year later, she had more than 200,000 fans, having attracted women in her daughter's age bracket, as well as in their 50s, 60s and 70s.

She also had major clothing, makeup and skincare brands knocking on her door to display their products online, as well as a talent agent and a contract to appear in a global ad campaign for Clairol.

"That's the beauty and joy of social media," she said, "we can connect and inspire each other."

Online creative success like Gym's, of course, is far from guaranteed, but in recent years it's become more feasible than you might think.

Platforms like TikTok and YouTube have grown more popular among older users, so brands seeking exposure in this demographic are increasingly following them there.

Retirement age creators, in turn, have been finding success in promoting commercial products alongside their personal tips on everything from fashion, cooking and grandparenting, to life lessons they've gathered over the years.

Mae Karwowski, founder of Obviously, an agency that connects companies with content creators, told the *New York Times*: "older influencers have popped in popularity...it's really been accelerating."

The creative marketplace, in essence, has been unshackled—where once only professional artists, performers, musicians, filmmakers and inventors were allowed access, the gates have now been thrown open to anyone, at any age, willing to give creative ventures a shot.

THE BIRTH OF A GAME CHANGE

Jack Conte was among the first to recognize the potential of this new frontier.

In 2005, he was a student at Stanford University when Steve Jobs, Apple's founder, gave a commencement speech in which he advised freshly minted graduates to: "Do what you believe is great work, and the only way to do great work is to love what you do. Don't settle."

Although Jack wasn't in attendance at Job's speech, he apparently absorbed the message and took it deeply to heart.

After earning a degree in music, with a unique focus on science and technology, Jack could easily have landed a job in the music or film industries or followed the traditional route of artists and songwriters—hit the club circuit, make a demo or album and try to land a music publishing or record deal.

Instead, he followed his bliss onto two internet platforms that were, at the time, just beginning to flourish.

Jack told me:

> *After college I started collecting guitars, accordions and old-world instruments, like Indian percussion instruments. And I just basically fell in love with sound. Then I started writing and recording, and within a few years I was making a living as a musician by uploading my music videos to YouTube and selling songs on iTunes.*

Jack was convinced that an internet-based creativity marketplace was an idea whose time had arrived. And he watched as three trends, he said, began converging to populate this environment with a "new creative class."

One of the big trends was the diminishing of costs and the lowering of barriers to entry for creative technologies like cameras, microphones, recording and video equipment. You could get into making studio quality movies and records for a thousand bucks. This was an incredible development that opened the doors to anyone who wanted to do high-quality creative work.

A second important trend was an increase in the number of distribution channels. It used to be that there was just ABC, CBS and NBC, and if you wanted to be seen or heard, you had to convince someone in a suit that you were worthy of one of those platforms.

Now, with the advent of the internet and services like Facebook, YouTube and Sound Cloud, there were millions of channels of distribution, so there was a democratization of fame.

Put these things together and what you had was a third trend, which was that you now had a bunch of people who could make amazing things and get them in front of other people.

I'm not sure people understood it yet, but this was the first time ever that this had been possible.

*It was cheap to make amazing things, and other
people could find these things very easily, no matter
where they were on the globe. It was an incredible,
amazing new phenomenon.*

IF YOU CREATE IT, THEY WILL COME

In 2013, witnessing what he believed was the future of
creativity as it emerged, Jack, his wife Nataly, and Sam
Yam, Jack's former college roommate, launched their own
phenomenon: *Patreon.com.*

Jack explained how this came about.

> *Over time, I realized that there were tens of millions
> of people around the world who wanted to be profes-
> sional creators and who now, because of the internet,
> could do that. But the problem was: how were those
> people going to be compensated for their time, energy
> and creative work? So I sketched out an idea for a
> solution.*
>
> *I said to myself: "What if, as a creator, I asked
> my fans for support? What if I just asked them for
> a buck a month? Like a membership platform, like
> PBS, NPR or any of these platforms where people
> pay a monthly membership fee to help the organi-
> zation continue to exist."*

I sat pondering this idea and got really excited about it, but I didn't have the guts to call anybody—I was too scared. But one afternoon I sat down with sheets of printer paper, and I sketched the whole thing out. Then I called up a bunch of folks who I thought could help me build it, and one of those people was Sam, my college roommate.

Jack's roommate, Sam, had studied engineering and computer science at Stanford, and was an expert at software coding and design, as well as a serial entrepreneur.

When I pitched the idea to Sam, he immediately got super excited about it. And that night, he started doing research and actually coding the whole website.

As this was happening, I realized that this concept was not just for YouTubers. It was also for journalists, podcasters, web comics or illustrators. It was for anybody who uploaded creative content to the web and needed to be paid for what they do— that was the realization.

And that was how Patreon came into existence.

In creating Patreon, Jack's vision was to link regular, everyday people with professional creators who were willing to provide an online window into ways in which they thought and worked.

As of summer 2023, Patreon's web portal had offered access to the web pages, videos and work of more than 260,000 creative professionals who, as a group, had attracted the financial support of some eight million patrons, from whom Patreon garnered commissions to fund its growing operations.

For Jack Conte, it was a vision come true.

For the first time in human history, it was possible to be a successful, viable, profitable creator who made creative things and distributed them online and make money from patronage. And this was not a promise anymore—it was a reality.

These individuals and companies were basically the small business version of a newspaper, or BuzzFeed or a Disney company. But instead of making billions of dollars and having millions of consumers who knew about them, they had thousands of people helping to support them, and they were running profitable, small, creative companies.

That's happening today, and we have the data to prove it.

SECRETS OF THE NEW CREATORS

One of the distinguishing characteristics of those who succeed in today's new creative marketplace is the way in which their lives, careers and businesses seamlessly blend.

Their work *supports* their way of life, the way they live *enhances* their work, and their creativity literally *is* their business which, if things go well, can be a source of significant income.

What if, in lieu of retirement, this sounds like the kind of new life adventure that might be right for you?

With this question in mind, I brought together three creators, from very different fields, who successfully made a go of it in the new online creative marketplace.

While they were considerably younger than retirement age, their experiences and advice could prove invaluable for anyone considering their style of life and work.

MEET SHAYLA, BRENDAN AND KATI

Shayla Mattox left behind an acting career to become a successful visual artist; Brendan Leonard quit his IBM marketing job to become a nationally known outdoor writer and author; Kati Morton, after entering private practice as a family therapist, went on to become, much to her surprise, the "Dr. Phil" of YouTube, Twitter and other social media.

I discovered them on Patreon.com, where each had posted videos about themselves and their work on their personal Patreon pages. As a result, in a 'techie' sort of way, I felt like I already knew them when we spoke in person.

In our conversation, I especially wanted to know the following:

How did they get started? What was their journey like? What advice might they provide to any of us interested in exploring and expressing our own creative potential?

What ideas, suggestions or guidance did they have to offer about navigating, and perhaps earning income, in today's new internet-based creative marketplace?

Why did they want to live and work in the way that they did?

Here's some of what I learned.

SHAYLA MADDOX
MIXED MEDIA ARTIST

Shayla Maddox was an accomplished Hollywood actress who, after years in the field, felt worn out and in need of a break. While "on sabbatical," as she characterized it, she picked up a paintbrush for the first time since her teen years and fell in love with making art all over again. She started showing her work in galleries and other locations, where people were sufficiently impressed to start buying and collecting it.

She never returned to Hollywood. "I loved painting so much," Shayla explained, "I decided that I felt like this is what I should be doing."

BRENDAN LEONARD
ADVENTURE WRITER WITH A TWIST

Brendan Leonard's professional life was an adventure from the start.

After graduating from college, he worked as a small-town newspaper columnist, earned a master's degree in journalism, was a salesman at REI and led backpacking trips before getting "a safe, well-paying job" as a marketing copywriter for IBM.

This was a predictably bad fit, given that Brendan's mind was generally elsewhere—on a mountainside or marathon running trail. While keeping his job, he started writing about the outdoors, with a unique focus on the humorous things that he and others experienced while pressing up against their physical limits.

Lots of funny things happen in the outdoor adventure world, but people weren't talking about

them back when I first got started. Everything was
sort of dead serious and, you know, about life and
death in the mountains and that kind of thing.

But there was a bunch of really humorous
material to work with—interpersonal moments
when you were ultra-running or rock climbing
that were hysterical. So, that's what I decided to
write about.

Within a year of its launch, Brendan's online blog began to take off, and magazine editors who'd previously ignored him began requesting articles, which he happily sold to them.

He also began self-publishing his own special brand of outdoorsy books, with titles like *The Art of Getting Lost*, and *Bears Don't Care about Your Problems* which, once publicized online, were surprisingly profitable.

KATI MORTON
"DR. PHIL" OF THE INTERNET

Kati Morton had never thought of herself as a creator until she gave it a try.

She was, by virtue of her training, a licensed marriage and family therapist with a specialty in eating disorders and self-harming behaviors—psychological maladies that intrigued her due to their complexity.

So no one was more shocked than Kati when she suddenly found herself with a huge following on YouTube, starring in on-camera presentations on topics ranging from trauma and abuse to personality disorders, anxiety and depression.

The last thing she ever expected was to become, as she put it, the internet's "modern day Dr. Phil."

> *I had never been into theater, acting or things like that. As a kid, I sang, but that's the closest I ever got to being in front of people. So just being comfortable on camera was a huge learning curve.*
>
> *A big part of my getting comfortable was realizing the connectivity the online space offers. YouTube allows me to help more people than I ever could in private practice.*

Not just for creative newbies like Kati but, for experienced creators at every level, becoming successful in today's new web-based creative marketplace has meant experimenting and sometimes struggling with new ways of being and working.

But, as you're about to read, the rewards in this new creative ecosystem, financial and otherwise, can outshine the investments.

In more than a few ways, the experience of becoming 21st century creators provided Shayla, Brendan and Kati with a sense of personal freedom and professional accomplishment beyond what they ever expected.

LEVERAGING THE NEW CREATIVE MARKETPLACE

Mark Walton: You were all early adopters. And, by that I mean, you were on the ground floor of the new creative marketplace, back when the now-giant web platforms, like YouTube and Facebook, were just getting going. What was that experience like for you, and how has it gone since—the good, bad and everything in-between?

Brendan (Adventure Writer): Personally, I would take this new world anytime over the way it was years ago, because a lot of the traditional gate-keepers have been minimized, if not eliminated. Before, I had to go through someone else to create a lot of the things that I did. Now I feel like I can create something in a couple of hours, and if people really like it, I can earn a few thousand dollars online. So I absolutely think it's right for me.

Shayla (Artist): First and foremost, I started my own webpage and blog, and that was the basic way people were getting onto the internet around 2004 or 2005. And, to my surprise, I just started selling paintings and couldn't believe it kept happening. So I think it's a lot easier now to be creative and make money than ever before.

Kati (YouTube Therapist): When I got out of school, a therapist had to gather 3,000 hours of clinical experience in California to become licensed. And, while I was doing that, my boyfriend told me about YouTube, and I thought: "No way, that sounds terrible. I don't want to be in the limelight, I don't want to be an actress, I don't like being on camera."

But, over the course of several months, he started sending me links to other YouTubers, and he said: "People do this for a living and it's a way to reach people." So I gave it a try, and I started looking at viewer comments and saw that the ability to reach people was truly amazing.

WHAT WOULD THEY ADVISE OTHERS?

Mark: What ideas, suggestions or guidance do you have for others, especially for people older than you, perhaps people who have had long careers as professionals, and are considering developing their creativity instead of retiring?

Kati Morton (YouTube Therapist): I believe we all know something worth sharing with others. My advice is to do it as simply as possible at first. If you don't have a lot of time, just shoot some videos on your phone, do the best run-through you can of information you want to get out there, and put it online. I think the more people we have sharing their expertise and knowledge, the better.

Brendan (Adventure Writer): In the beginning, before I started doing this full-time, I kept my day job and worked on creative stuff on the side until I was able to make a go of it. I think that's the safe way to try something, and it allows you to slowly grow a creative business without a lot of pressure. Most people's creative careers don't take off overnight, or even over the span of a year, so don't be afraid to try, because the price for failing is so low.

Shayla (Artist): I definitely recommend jumping in to be a creator. Become obsessed with it, that's what you need to do. It's probably better to start out following a lot of artists, or other creators, on Patreon.com. Follow their journey and see what you can learn from them for a period of time while working on building your own fan base and community.

HOW CREATIVITY PAYS THEM BACK

Mark: *You all seem to be making a go of it, financially. Other than that, what else does being creative provide you? That is, are there other ways that your work pays you back?*

Shayla (Artist): *Oh, goodness, I can get very emotional about this. This is such a huge and wondrous thing for me that, even if I was not getting paid, I would still feel that I was succeeding at something and doing something important. I get letters from kids sometimes who absolutely love my art and are inspired and want to be an artist when they grow up. So that's very emotional and profound for me.*

Kati (YouTube Therapist): *Yeah, I agree 100%. Obviously, there is a great feeling when a patient in your office finally realizes something you've been trying to get them to see for, perhaps, years. But online there's also an aha moment. It comes when I'm impacting people by putting out content and*

*educating people about what I know. To me, that's
a joy that means everything.*

Brendan (Adventure Writer): *I get emails and
an occasional letter from people who will say: "This
thing you created, your book, whatever, turned my
life around or informed the way I live." A guy once
wrote me and said: "I have a master's degree from a
pretty big-name university, but I've battled dyslexia
my entire life, and your book about climbing and
addiction is the first book I've ever finished." And
that really impacted me in a major way.*

TAKING CREATIVITY OFF THE PEDESTAL

Because Kati Morton had been the least creatively experienced of the group when she first insecurely ventured
out and then stumbled into creative success, I was struck
by the final thoughts she shared as we wrapped up
our conversation.

*I once heard someone say, and now I know this from
personal experience, that we need to take creativity
off a pedestal. Everybody acts like: "Oh, I'm not
creative, I can't do that, that's something that a
creative person would do." Well, that's nonsense.*

I think we're all naturally creative. We just need to take creativity off a pedestal and get started on something that we will enjoy creating.

"No matter our age or stage of life," Kati made a point of adding, as she, Brendan and Shayla headed back to work in the new creative marketplace.

CHAPTER FOURTEEN

Changing the Map of Life

On the wall of her modest office in Berkeley, California was a small plaque with a quotation from the Gospel of Thomas that read: "If you bring forth what is within you, what you bring forth will save you. If you do not bring forth what is within you, what you do not bring forth will destroy you."

These were the words that animated Marion Rosen's life and most especially her three decades in unretirement.

They were the message behind the smile in her eyes, the unique work that she developed over her lifetime and the global phenomenon that carries her name today.

The first time I visited with Marion, shortly before her 92nd birthday, she recalled how unlikely it had once seemed that things would turn out this way.

When I was about 55 and I was a physical therapist, the doctors who had been sending me patients were retiring or dying, so I thought I would just wait until I got social security and sit down and wait until I died.

That's what I had thought would happen. But it didn't happen, and now that it didn't happen, I'm just as happy to go on doing what I love to do until I really die. When I can't work anymore, I might consider dying.

Marion's initial pessimism about the future was understandable, given the difficult lessons she learned about loss early in life.

As a Jewish teenager in pre-war Germany, she was banned from movie theaters, restaurants and attending college—former friends, including a special boyfriend, turned their backs on her.

Yet somehow, in the darkness, as the Nazi party rose to power, Marion found a shining light.

In her early 20s, Marion's mother scheduled an appointment for her with a Munich massage therapist named Lucy Heyer, who worked with her husband, Gustav, a practicing psychoanalyst.

On the massage table in their office, Marion discovered a fascination that would never fade.

I came there with migraine headaches, which got really bad. And she put her hands on me, and the way she touched me, something happened, and the headache went away. And I felt different, very good, and I remember thinking: "I'm going to learn this work and do it the rest of my life."

I stayed there and I trained with her. And the way she trained me was that she worked on me and she let me watch her working on others, and then she had me work on others. Most of her patients were also patients of her husband. And they had discovered that, when these patients had physical treatments along with psychological treatments, the psychological treatments went much deeper and faster.

Soon, as Hitler's stormtroopers began to unleash their "final solution," raiding homes, burning synagogues and transporting tens of thousands of Jews to concentration camps, Marion and her family managed to escape.

She settled first in England, then in Stockholm, then traveled on to America, where she trained at the Mayo Clinic in Minnesota before starting a 30-year career as a licensed physical therapist in the San Francisco area.

During those years, while treating injured factory workers and wounded American soldiers, in tandem with her mainstream physical therapy techniques, Marion would often apply what she had learned in Germany about the connection between mind and body.

While treating patients by hand, she asked probing questions: *How did this injury occur? What memories come up when I put my hand here? How does this affect your pain?*

Concerned about jeopardizing her professional credentials, she did this quietly and judiciously at first.

But, over time, she increasingly came to see that her patients were impacted not only by physical injuries, but also by emotional experiences from the past—that memories could be unconsciously fused into their bodies and later manifest as restricted movement and physical pain.

"We hold our anger back." Marion said. "We hold our sadness back. We use certain muscles in our body to suppress certain emotions."

As Helen Morgan, one of Marion's patients, told me: "there was just something about the way she talked with people, how she worked with people on what's deep inside, covered over or hidden, that made a big difference."

When Marion reached her mid-50s, as referring physicians retired or passed away, her patient pipeline began to dry up. And it was only by bringing her unconventional treatments into the limelight that she saved herself from a meager retirement.

A 35-YEAR UNRETIREMENT

The turning point was a phone call from a 22-year-old named Sara Webb, who had been fired from her position as a middle school teacher, her first job out of college.

Sara's brother had suffered from asthma, had been treated by Marion and, after a few sessions, had seen his asthma disappear.

Sara later told me:

I was looking for something in a career that was more exciting to me and more interesting. My mother had thought that maybe Marion would be willing to teach me some of what she knew, and maybe I could start a new career from that.

So I followed my mother's suggestion and called Marion and then went and knocked on the door at her physical therapy office. And we must have talked for an hour, even though the first thing she said to me was: "No, I'm not a teacher."

But a day later, she called and said that she had given it some thought, and she was willing to meet again and talk some more.

Marion took a liking to Sara, began to share her methods with her, and Sara soon started to bring other people along.

I brought my friends for Marion to show me how to work on them, and then they brought everybody they knew. This was the early 1970s, you know, and there was a real hunger for this kind of thing in California.

The hunger was not just among Sara's friends—as word spread, clinical psychologists, physical therapists and professional dancers lined up to learn Marion's techniques as well.

Consequently, at age 66, Marion selected the first participants for a multi-year training curriculum at the newly launched Rosen Institute in Berkeley. Over the following decade, Rosen training centers spread across the U.S., Western Europe, Israel, Australia and Canada.

By the time Marion reached age 86, there were more than 2,000 Rosen Method practitioners and teachers worldwide, along with books, CDs, videos and an online journal of research derived from Marion's sessions with patients, which she never stopped providing.

Sara, who over the years played a variety of roles in the Rosen organization, observed that, as Marion grew older, she seemed more dedicated and enlivened by her work all the time.

I don't think it felt like hard work to her. Dealing with all the business that went with it sometimes was difficult, but teaching and seeing people grow and expand was really music to her ears.

And the faces—she always spoke about seeing people's faces light up and that she could walk into a room at the end of a class and see that it had been a good class just by looking at people's faces. So that really fed her.

I remember her saying that's why she lived so long. I mean, she could really see how what she had done was making a difference in the world.

On my final visit with Marion, several years before her death, her voice was a bit softer, her walk less certain than when we first met, but the happiness remained in her soft blue eyes.

Of all the things she had experienced and learned over time, I asked, what had proven to be the key to her long and clearly happy life?

It's working more, more work—because this is active, it is using yourself. It's like you have a bicycle, and if it stands there and you don't use it, it rusts, it doesn't work anymore. But if you work it all the time, it starts, it works fine and the wheels turn. Our wheels turn better when we work, when we are alive, when we are part of whatever goes on.

I work, I give out what's in me, and I have very few physical complaints for my age, very few. Because this is what life is about, I think. That you will do what you can do and that you have to use everything in you in order to fulfill your life. That's really it, you have to give it all.

I would not want to live a retirement life. Living that way would be tragic. It's so wonderful to be my age and have experienced what I have and still be wanted, to be asked to share it and really have something to offer.

To give that up—it's inconceivable.

Marion never gave up her work—she continued to teach and treat patients until she suffered a stroke in December 2011 and passed away a month later at age 97.

A NEW MAP OF LIFE

Demographers tell us that there will come a time, not long from now, when a 10-decade lifespan like Marion Rosen's will be commonplace—the result of the cumulative advances in healthcare, sanitation, diet, lifestyle and technology that originated in the 20th century and continue today.

In fact, Stanford University, a short drive from where Marion lived and worked, has created a special center to study all of this and draw up a blueprint for what they term "century lives."

"Our ancestors in the early 20th century handed us a gift of roughly 30 extra years of life," explained Professor Laura Carstensen, who heads up this effort, "but what we did with these years is tack them all on at the end, so the only stage that got longer was old age. And it's not working for people; it's not working well at all."

The solution, according to the center's researchers, is to design a "New Map of Life," one that spreads out and reallocates time in the different stages of a lifetime.

For example, Carstensen proposes, "make elementary school a little bit longer, make work four days a week, and you find that people are living higher quality lives and people are happier."

The center's prototype design, available on its website, is filled with all sorts of multicolored diagrams that feature dotted lines and miniature traffic signs directing the flow of life from here to there.

The problem with this, I think, is that living is not an academic exercise—it's fired at us point blank, and there's no "time out" to ponder, discuss or remix its ingredients as if it were an apple pie.

If there is to be a new map of life—which clearly there must be, given our increasing longevity—my sense is that it is already organically evolving and can readily be seen if we look in the right places.

It's happening in the halls of the Mayo Clinic, where late 70 and 80-year-old physicians and researchers continue to advance the practice of medicine; inside companies like Vistage Worldwide, where age and experience have become integral parts of the business plan; in venues where the artwork, music, photography, fashion design and other creative pursuits of octogenarians and beyond are on display; and in the new businesses and reinventive careers of the rapidly growing millions of happily unretired people across the American landscape.

Perhaps someday you will join them.

NOTES

Introduction

1. *Like I said:* Vito Maggiolo in personal interview with the author.
2. *Most of the people:* W. James DeMartini M.D., in personal interview with the author.
3. *Between the years:* Sarah Flood, Miriam King, Renae Rodgers, Steven Ruggles, J. Robert Warren and Michael Westberry. *Integrated Public Use Microdata Series, Current Population Survey: Version 10.0* [dataset]. Minneapolis, MN: IPUMS, 2022.
4. *And the numbers:* Flood et al. ibid.
5. *By the year 2030:* U.S. Census Bureau Projections
6. *What's more:* Pew Research Center Report "Older Workers Are Growing in Number and Earning Higher Wages," December 14, 2023.
7. *For many people:* Demetria Gallegos, "When Will I Retire? How About Never," *Wall Street Journal*, April 20, 2023.
8. *We are entering:* Ewan Thomson, "The Rise of Unretirement," *World Economic Forum*, www.weforum.org, June 30, 2023.

Chapter One

1. *I think the worst part:* Robert Pascale PhD, in personal interview with the author.
2. *There's always:* Louis Primavera PhD, in personal interview with the author.

Chapter Two

1. *I can't understand:* Alyce Shultz, RN, PhD, in personal interview with the author.

2. *Today this approach:* "What is Evidence Based Practice in Nursing?" *American Nurses Association*, www.nursingworld.org/practice.

Chapter Three

1. *I liked winning:* Robert Delamontagne in personal interview with the author.

2. *You slam:* Robert Delamontagne, PhD, *The Retiring Mind*, Fairview Imprints, 2010, pg. 18.

3. *I had a nice:* Susan Nolingberg in personal interview with the author.

Chapter Four

1. *Sometimes I feel:* Dalai Lama in "The Mayo Clinic - Faith, Hope, Science," *PBS Documentary*, September, 2018.

2. *I love what I do:* Chet Rihal M.D., in personal interview with the author.

3. *Dr. Will went:* Helen Clapesattle, *The Doctors Mayo*, Mayo Foundation for Medical Education and Research, 1990, pg. 413.

4. *Every physician:* Mark Truty M.D., PBS Documentary, op. cit.

5. *If you had asked:* Thomas Habermann M.D., in personal interview with the author.

6. *Some people:* Ronald Petersen M.D., in personal interview with the author.

7. *Showed she still:* James Clark, "Stevie Nicks Caps a Bonnaroo for the Ages," *Southern Standard,* June 20, 2022.

8. *Nothing makes me:* Rachel DeSantis, "Ringo Starr Says Nothing Makes Me Feel Old," *People magazine*, July 4, 2023.

9. *He inherited:* Ruth Johnson M.D., in personal interview with the author.

10. *I have an older:* Ronald Petersen M.D., Ibid.

11. *Love and work:* Jeremy E. Sherman PhD., "Love, Work, Play," *Psychology Today*, December 13, 2009.

Chapter Five

1. *Dear Friend: Steven A. Holmes,* "The World According to AARP," *New York Times*, March 21, 2001.

2. *My dad used to say:* Horace Deets in personal interview with the author.

3. *The American Association: AARP Press Room*, press.aarp.org.

4. *The solution:* Jennifer Mann, "Sensing an Image Problem, AARP Ditches Full Name," *Pueblo Chieftan*, February 27, 1999.

5. *They think they're going:* Ibid.

6. *Of all the challenges:* Steven A. Holmes, op. cit.

7. *My first recollection:* Mitch Anthony in personal interview with the author.

8. *Money can find purpose:* Mitch Anthony, *The New Retirementality*, Wiley, 2019.

9. *W-O-R-K is no:* Mitch Anthony speech to Financial Planners Association, 2014.

10. *The financial services:* Marc Freedman, *Encore: Finding Work that Matters in the Second Half of Life*, Public Affairs, 2000.

11. *I think when people:* Marc Freedman in personal interview with the author.

12. *I had done:* Ruth Wooden in personal interview with the author.

Chapter Six

13. *Forty years in the:* Peter F. Drucker, *Management Challenges for the 21st Century*, HarperBusiness, 1999, pp. 188-194.

14. *This perspective:* Michael M. Merzenich, *Society for Neuroscience,* www.sfn.org.

15. *We're continuously plastic:* Michael Merzenich in personal interview with the author.

16. *Frequently when:* Elkhonon Goldberg PhD, *The Wisdom Paradox: How Your Mind Can Grow Stronger As Your Brain Grows Older,* Gotham Books, 2005, pg. 9.

17. *And this is what:* Elkhonon Goldberg in personal interview with the author.

Chapter Seven

1. *They offered*: Kerry Hannon in personal interview with the author.

2. *In May of*: "Stepping into the Future: Employers, Workers and the Multigenerational Workforce, *Transamerica Institute*, May 2023, www.transamericainstitute.org.

3. *The creative control:* Mark Miller in personal interview with the author.

4. *Experts caution*: Mark Miller, "How A Solo Gig Can Give You A Stronger Retirement," *New York Times,* May 15, 2023.

5. *Over recent decades:* "Trends in Entrepreneurship Series," *E.M. Kaufmann Foundation,* April 2021, www.kaufmann.org.

Chapter Eight

1. *That whole period:* Mona Stallworth in personal interview with the author.

Chapter Nine

1. *I'm no longer:* Ken Mandelbaum in personal interview with the author.

2. *Let me give*: Jeanette Hobson in personal interview with the author.

3. *The first three:* Sam Reese in personal interview with the author.

4. *I think people:* Kevin Trout in personal interview with the author.

5. *Today it is possible:* Warren Bennis and James O'Toole, *Harvard Business Review,* May 2005.

6. *A few B-school faculty:* Warren Bennis, "Have Business Schools Found their Way?"

7. www.bloomberg.com, July 9, 2012.

8. *Ten years after:* Jon Eckhart and James Wetherbe, "Making Business School Research More Relevant," *Harvard Business Review,* December 2014.

Chapter Ten

1. *It's not for us:* Candace Kahn in personal interview with the author.

2. *I don't even:* Larry Kahn in personal interview with the author.

Chapter Eleven

1. *From here on*: Sherwin B. Nuland, *"The Art of Aging,"* Random House, 2007, pp. 10-11.

2. *I've never thought:* Sherwin B. Nuland in personal interview with the author.

Chapter Twelve

1. *The loggers*: Rita Spina in personal interview with the author.

2. *Of course we do:* Michael Merzenich in personal interview with the author.

3. *I had started:* Gil Garcetti in personal interview with the author.

Chapter Thirteen

1. *My career didn't*: Abigail Cuffey, "Gym Tan On Being A TikTok Influencer at Age 62," *Women's Health,* February 14, 2023, www.womenshealthmag.com.

2. *Older influencers:* Julie Weed, "As Older TikTok Creators Flourish, Brands Are Signing Them Up," *New York Times,* June 3, 2023.

3. *After college:* Jack Conte in personal interview with the author.

4. *I loved painting:* Shayla Maddox in personal interview with the author.

5. *There's a lot of funny*: Brendan Leonard in personal interview with the author.

6. *I had never been*: Kati Morton in personal interview with the author.

Chapter Fourteen

1. *When I was about:* Marion Rosen in personal interview with the author.

2. *There was just:* Helen Morgan in personal interview with the author.

3. *I was looking:* Sara Webb in personal interview with the author.

4. *Our ancestors:* Laura Carstensen PhD, *21st Century Summit,* longevity.stanford.edu.

Author's note: Personal interviews featured in the book were recorded, transcribed, lightly edited and condensed for clarity and flow.

APPENDIX

Below are excerpts from a speech on unretirement by Mortimer J. Adler, widely regarded as one of America's leading Aristotelian philosophers, at the annual meeting of the "Million Dollar Roundtable" of the National Association of Insurance Underwriters on July 16, 1962.

Adler spoke following an opulent breakfast at the luxurious Queen Elizabeth Hotel in Montreal, Canada, one of the world's first hotels to feature air conditioning and private telephones in each of its 1200 rooms.

Prior to his presentation to top performers in the insurance industry, previous guests of the hotel had included Queen Elizabeth, the Duke of Edinburgh, Princess Grace, Charles de Gaulle and Fidel Castro.

"THE PARTS OF LIFE"
BY MORTIMER J. ADLER

Members of the Million Dollar Round Table: I am deeply sensible of the honor you have bestowed upon me by inviting me to address you.

I do not know all the intricacies of your profession, but I am assuming that life insurance is concerned with the living as well as with the dead. Therefore, it is the aspect of life which one can insure that is the center of my consideration this morning.

Let me begin by calling your attention to the simple fact that we are living in an extraordinary, revolutionary period.

We live in a society, an environment, in which, for the first time in history, change is so rapid that, as Margaret Mead has aptly pointed out, none of us dies in the world in which he was born. The world has completely changed. Our grandfathers and great grandfathers died in a world which in all significant respects had remained almost identical with the world in which they were born.

We live in a society in which most men have more free time than any group of men ever had in the past. And, finally, we live in a society in which the advances of medical science and art have increased the length of life. Increased longevity is a fundamental fact and a fundamental fact of interest to you.

Today all of us must think how best to use our wealth, since we all have sufficient wealth; or how best to use our free time, since we all have more free time than we know what to do with. And we all face the even more important problem of how best to prepare for old age and retirement.

I want to say at once that these two problems are closely connected, for, in fact, the age at which we now retire from earning a living can hardly be described as senility. It is an age at which men now achieve their full growth or maturity; and the problem we face is what to do with our maturity when we have retired from earning a living.

The shape the problem of retirement takes for us is determined by a number of things: by the fact of the increasing numbers of men who can or must retire, by the fact that the retirement age is coming down from 70 to 68 to 65 to 60 and may, in the course of the next 25 or 50 years, go below that, and by an additional fact, which complicates the matter considerably: that life gets longer, that retirement is something which happens in the prime of life, not in old age, not in feebleness.

Retirement is a long stretch of free time in what is the prime of life, characterized by exemption from work, that is, from earning a living. We are faced with the same old question: What shall we do with that free time?

Retirement conceived as a protracted vacation is a form of suicide. No animal, and man is an animal, retires from activity without dying. Dr. Theodore Klump, a noted heart specialist, in an article printed in the IBM magazine, *Think*, said: "I believe we must do everything we can, as we grow older, to resist the inclination to slow down the tempo of our living." Otherwise, we will be engaged in a slow retreat into oblivion.

He went on to say: "I am convinced that one who just sits and waits for death to come along will not have long to wait, for we don't wear out, we rust out." Finally, he said: "Throughout the realm of living things, nature tends to eliminate those that have relinquished their functional usefulness." Men relinquish theirs when retirement takes the form of a permanent vacation. That amounts to giving up all functional usefulness and is a form of self-elimination or suicide.

This is not only wrong biologically, but also morally. For what justifies recreation except a need to refresh oneself from toil or from leisure, from activities that impose strains and fatigue upon the body or the mind?

If you are not engaged in anything that involves strain and fatigue, what right have you to recreate yourself? What right have you to refresh yourself continually? You always retain the right to play moderately, but a life full of recreation, full of play, is not morally justified, and idleness or time killing is one of the seven deadly sins, sloth.

It is not only morally and biologically wrong, but also *psychologically*, because everyone knows how boring a vacation can become if it is too protracted. Retirement, thus constituted, would involve the boredom or vacancy of a permanent and unending vacation. Please note that the word "vacation" has the same root as the word "vacancy."

What is the right answer to this very difficult question, but it is this: that retirement should be a transition from toil to what Aristotle characterized as *leisure work*, that is leisure time that contains the true goods of life.

Robert Browning, in that great poem of his, *Rabbi Ben Ezra*, wrote: "Grow old along with me, the best is yet to be, the last of life for which the first was made." That describes an advance, not a recession, *the last of life for which the first was made.* [Retirement should be a transition to pure *leisure work*: to government, to teaching, to creative activities of one kind or another, to learning or study, or even to some form of subsistence work with a leisure aspect and without extrinsic compensation.]

This last point is important because retirement is economically required to enable young men to climb up the ladder. I see nothing wrong with a banker remaining a banker at a dollar a year if banking interests him as a leisure activity, nor anything wrong with an executive vice president of an industrial corporation remaining executive vice-president if he does not earn a living doing that, but rather engages in the activity for the leisure involved in it, for the contribution that he thereby makes to society and to himself.

If his ordinary day-to-day job has a leisure aspect, let him continue to do it without compensation, or let him turn to other activities.

When you understand retirement in this way, you realize that "retirement" is a bad word for a good idea. [I wish we could retire the word "retirement" itself; for the word "retirement" suggests *inactivity*, going on the shelf or into the discard or lapsing into idleness. The right word should be "graduation," moving up, stepping up from a lower to higher grade of life.]

My friend Clarence Randall said, when he retired as head of Inland Steel and went into government service, that he had graduated. He was stepping up, not down. He was not retiring, he was graduating to a better, a more important, mode of life.

If retirement is to be truly a graduation, how does one prepare for it? How does one school oneself for it?

If, during the years of making a living, all of an individual's free time has been devoted to play or recreation, that individual is totally unprepared for retirement as graduation; he is prepared only for demotion to the progressive emptiness of a life of play or vacation, not for graduation to a fuller, richer life.

If retirement, properly understood, is a graduation, then the preparation for it lies in forms of leisure work that one engages in during the free time that one has in the years of working or making a living.

If we postpone everything that is important during the years when we have so many urgent things to do, we will never be ready for the important things when all the urgencies have disappeared. During the years when we are occupied with the urgency of business, we must give sufficient attention to the important things of life, not play, in order to occupy our last years with nothing but important things.

Professor L. D. Cory, at the 10th Annual Gerontological Conference, said that a successful adjustment to retirement appears to depend on how long the individual has gone to school. The better one's education, the better the adjustment.

I would go further than that and say that the more real learning an individual engages in during the working years of his adult life, the better his solution to the problem of how to live well in the years when work is done.

What a man has learned to do well between the ages of 25 and 50 or 60, he can continue to do well after 50 or 60 for many years to come.

Reprinted by permission of the Center for the Study of Great Ideas

ACKNOWLEDGEMENTS

In the process of researching and writing *Unretired*, I happened upon a community— a group much larger and significant than today's print, broadcast or cable media might lead us to believe exists.

It's an entire society, in fact, of people who passionately subscribe to Ernest Hemingway's words quoted at the beginning of this volume: ["Retirement is the filthiest word in the language. Whether by choice or fate, to retire from what you do—and what makes you what you are—is to back up into the grave."]

Without these individuals, and those who introduced me to them, this book would not have been possible, for they provided me the real-life case studies and first-person insights with which to document and explain the rapidly growing trend toward unretirement that is changing the map of our lives.

I am grateful to every one of them.

At the Mayo Clinic, they include masterful physicians and researchers Robert D. Brown, Charanjit S. Rihal,

Thomas M. Habermann, Ronald C. Petersen, Ruth Johnson, Vanda A. Lennon and communication specialist Susan M. Barber Linquist.

At Vistage Worldwide, I extend my appreciation to Mary-Jo Lipman, Sam Reese, Kevin Trout, Jeanette Hobson, Ken Mandelbaum, Janet Fogarty, Jean Lauterbach and Katie McWeeney.

For their invaluable assistance with the demographic statistics around which this book revolves, I owe shout outs to Matthew Rutledge at the Boston College Center for Retirement Research and Richard Fry at the Pew Research Center.

And there are many more special people, in a variety of careers and organizations, to whom I send thanks, including Vito Maggiolo, Robert Delamontagne, Alyce and Teri Schultz, Susan Nolingberg, Mona Stallworth, Michael Merzenich, Elkhonon Goldberg, Rob Pascale, Lou Primavera, Larry and Candace Kahn, Mark Miller, Kerry Hannon, Jim DeMartini, Mitch Anthony, Marc Freedman, Sara Webb, Gil Garcetti, Jack Conte, Shayla Maddox, Brendan Leonard and Kati Morton.

And while they are no longer with us, in memoriam I want to acknowledge my indebtedness to Shep Nuland, Rita Spina and Marion Rosen.

At Profit Research, Inc., the venerable New York financial publishing house, I benefited greatly from the expertise of Marjorie Marks and her outstanding team; also not to be forgotten is my extraordinary independent designer, Ivica Jandrijević, who helped to bring the concept of *Unretired* to life.

Each time I've tackled a challenging journalistic project such as this one, I've been supported by the love, patience and perseverance of my wife, Jane, the best managing editor I've ever known, and by the memory of my father, the late Sidney Walton—writer, broadcast pioneer and publisher extraordinaire, both of whom are my north stars on the long days and middle-of-the-nights when I'm waiting for the right words to appear.

ABOUT THE AUTHOR

Mark S. Walton is a Peabody award-winning journalist, Fortune 100 management consultant, and Chairman of the Center for Leadership Communication, a global executive education and communication enterprise with a focus on leadership and exceptional achievement at every stage of life.

In his role as the Center's founder and chairman he has taught, coached, and advised thousands of leaders, managers and career professionals in corporate universities and executive programs at many of the world's leading organizations including: Bank of America, Dow Chemical, General Electric Corporation, Duke Energy, Toyota Motor Corporation, GlaxoSmithKline, NASA, and the United States Navy and Marine Corps.

In 2017, he established the Second Half Institute, a new division of the Center, which provides university based and public programs in career renewal and rein-vention for accomplished executives and professionals in midcareer and beyond.

Mark is the Amazon bestselling author of *Boundless Potential: Transform Your Brain, Unleash Your Talents, Reinvent Your Work in Midlife and Beyond* (McGraw-Hill) on which the nationwide PBS-TV Special, "*Boundless Potential with Mark Walton,*" was based. His previous book was *Generating Buy-In: Mastering the Language of Leadership, which was* published by the American Management Association, and selected by Soundview Executive Summaries as one of the Top 30 business books of the year.

Earlier in his career, he was CNN's first Chief White House Correspondent and later CNN Senior Correspondent and Anchor, traveling the globe from network headquarters in Atlanta, reporting on live breaking news as well as political, social and business trends.

He is a recipient of broadcast journalism's premier honor, the George Foster Peabody Award, as well as the National Headliner Award, Ohio State Journalism Award, Cable Ace Award, Gold Medal of the New York TV and Film Festival and the Silver Gavel of the American Bar Association.

Mark can be reached by email at leadercommunication @earthlink.net or via his corporate website at www. secondhalfinstitute.com.

Printed in the USA
CPSIA information can be obtained
at www.ICGtesting.com
LVHW041014150524
780332LV00008B/527